The Timeless Path

The Timeless Path

A Step-by-Step Guide to Spiritual Evolution

Swami Ramakrishnananda Puri

Mata Amritanandamayi Center
San Ramon, California, United States

The Timeless Path:
A Step-by-Step Guide to Spiritual Evolution
By Swami Ramakrishnananda Puri

Published By:
Mata Amritanandamayi Center
P.O. Box 613, San Ramon, CA 94583-0613 USA

In India:
www.amritapuri.org
inform@amritapuri.org

In USA:
www.amma.org

In Europe:
www.amma-europe.org

Dedication

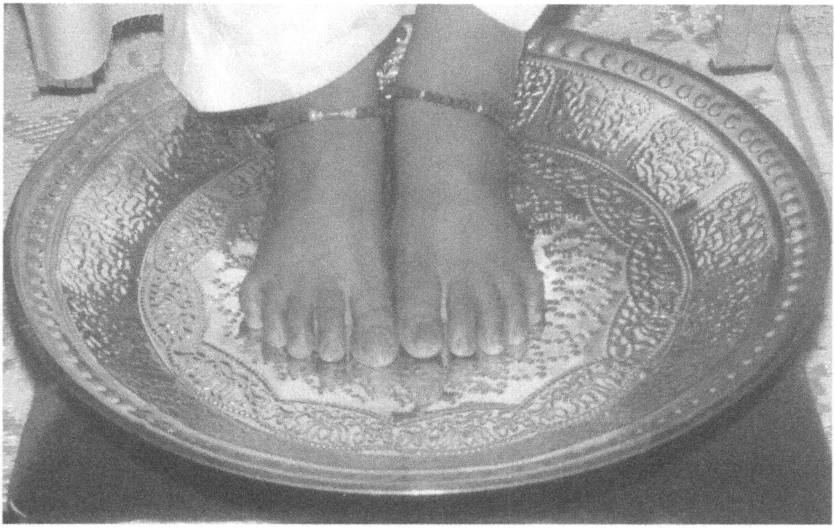

I humbly offer this book at the Lotus Feet of my Sadguru,
Śrī Mātā Amṛtānandamayi Devī.

Table of Contents

Preface:

The Timeless Path

O Goddess, so that I may come to live in your presence,
please lead me along this timeless path.
Enchantress of the universe, please guide me always.
O embodiment of consciousness, existence and bliss,
I am bowing to you with folded hands.

—from the bhajan 'En Mahādevi Lokeśi Bhairavi'
by Amma

SPRITUALITY IS OFTEN referred to as a path. But where does it actually begin and where does it end? Where does it take us? Furthermore, who actually lays it? Is the seeker himself the trail-blazer—hacking through the jungle with his lone machete? Or is it laid out before us, cleared by past masters? Are there multiple paths or just one? And as Amma's children, what exactly is the path she is laying out before us? If spiritual life really is a journey, then these are all important questions.

In the *bhajan* that serves as the epigraph to this preface, Amma prays to Devi to lead her along the *śāśvata mārga*. Śāśvata means 'eternal'; mārga means 'path.' But we should not take 'eternal' as indicating that the path has no end. What Amma means is that the spiritual path itself is *timeless*—that, for every generation, in every cycle of creation, it remains the same.

Hinduism is often referred to as Sanātana Dharma—the Eternal Way of Life. This is because the Vedas, the primary scriptures detailing the spiritual path, are said to be *anādi*—without beginning—and *ananta*—always existing. The Vedas are not human creations but an eternal part of the universe—as some poetically put it, 'the breath of God.' In each cycle of creation, they are not formulated anew, but rather 'dawn' in the minds of saints and sages—men and women of minds so purified that the Vedic *mantras* and truths appear to them as if written on the very wind. It is these men and women who pass the Vedas down to the first disciples. Thus they continue being handed down, from generation to generation, in an endless lineage.

In this book we will explore this Timeless Path, closely examining its major twists and turns. We will also see that, despite the fact Amma has never studied the scriptures, the path inculcated by her is the same as the one presented in the Vedas and recapitulated in subsequent traditional scriptures such as the Bhagavad-Gīta. As Amma once said to a reporter who asked her what her teaching was, "My path is the path of Śrī Kṛṣṇa[1]; there is nothing new here."

Through this book, we will see that what many consider to be so many different paths—*karma yoga*, meditation, *jñāna yoga*, etc.—are all in fact various aspects of one path. As Amma often says, "*Karma* [action], *jñāna* [knowledge] and *bhakti* [devotion] are all essential. If the two wings of a bird are devotion and action, knowledge is its tail. Only with the help of all three can the bird soar into the heights." Karma yoga and practices like meditation propel spiritual seekers forward, while the wisdom of the masters gives us the proper direction.

Someone like Amma, with true spiritual vision, accepts all religions, understanding the proper place their practices have in the grand scheme of the one path. As Amma explained at the General Assembly of the United Nations in New York in 2000, "The goal of all religions is one—purification of the human mind."

The Hindus have their systems for mental purification, the Buddhists theirs, the Christians theirs, so too the Jews, Jains and

[1] "Kṛṣṇa's path" as presented in the Bhagavad-Gīta was a recapitulation of the Vedic path.

Muslims, etc. Sanātana Dharma accepts them all. But ultimately, after the mind is rendered pure, the spiritual seeker must transcend all such practices and come to understand his true nature. For it is only in this that the seeker reaches the end of the Timeless Path. After all, like the Vedas and the path enumerated by them, spiritual ignorance is also said to be without beginning. But unlike the Vedas, ignorance does have an end. It comes with the blissful understanding that what is truly timeless, in fact, is our own Self.

Śrī Mātā Amṛtānandamayi Devī

"As long as there is enough strength to reach out to those who come to me, to place my hand on a crying person's shoulder, Amma will continue to give darśan.To lovingly caress people, to console and wipe their tears until the end of this mortal frame—this is Amma's wish."

—Amma

THROUGH HER EXTRAORDINARY acts of love and self-sacrifice, Śrī Māta Amṛtānandamayi Devi, or 'Amma' [Mother], as she is more commonly known, has endeared herself to millions around the world. Tenderly caressing everyone who comes to her, holding them close to her heart in a loving embrace, Amma shares her boundless love with all—regardless of their beliefs, their status, or why they have come to her. In this simple yet powerful way, Amma is transforming the lives of countless people, helping their hearts to blossom, one embrace at a time. In the past 37 years, Amma has physically hugged more than 29 million people from all parts of the world.[1]

Her tireless spirit of dedication to uplifting others has inspired a vast network of charitable activities, through which people are discovering the deep sense of peace and inner fulfillment that comes from selflessly serving others. Amma teaches that the divine exists in everything, sentient and insentient. Realizing this truth is the essence of spirituality—the means to end all suffering.

Amma's teachings are universal. Whenever she is asked about her religion, she replies that her religion is love. She does not ask anyone to believe in God or to change their faith, but only to inquire into their own real nature and to believe in themselves.

---

[1] Figures as of first printing, 2009

Chapter One:

Why People Come to Amma

"Just as our bodies need proper food to live and develop, our souls need love to blossom. The strength and nourishment that love can give our souls is even more potent than the nourishing power of a mother's milk for a baby."

—Amma

IF YOU ATTEND one of Amma's programs, one of the first things you will notice is that people come to Amma from everywhere—from all religions, all countries, all walks of life. Some have been walking the spiritual path for decades; others have never even picked up a spiritual book in their lives. Some come because they are suffering mentally, physically or materially, and they hope Amma can help them. Some are simply curious. Perhaps they have seen Amma in the newspaper or on the TV, and they want to see for themselves what this 'Hugging Saint' thing is all about. Then there are the seekers—both novices and adepts. They believe Amma, being an enlightened spiritual master, can take them to the ultimate goal of human life—Self-realization.

The majority of people come to see Amma because they have some problem and they hope she can fix it. In the Bhagavad-Gīta, Kṛṣṇa refers to people who come to God or a *mahātma* to be rescued from dire straits as *ārtas*. At the beginning of her public talks, Amma often begins by addressing these people, saying, "Amma knows that 90 percent of the people here are suffering physically or emotionally. Some don't have a job. Others have jobs but need raises. Others are unable to find suitors for their daughters. Some others are involved in legal cases. Some don't have the money to buy a house. Others have houses but can't sell them. Some have incurable diseases..." Amma tells these people that there is no point in worrying, that to do so is like simply looking at a wound and crying. She tells them that worry only exacerbates the situation and that what needs to be done is to apply medicine. She advises them to put in their best effort and then surrender to God's will, allowing him to carry the weight of their burdens.

Indeed many of these people do find that their problems are remedied to various extents. Women who have never been able to conceive children suddenly find themselves pregnant. People embroiled in legal battles who pray to Amma often find the balance swinging in their favor. Financial problems are alleviated. There have even been cases where physical ailments either diminish or completely subside. When presented with this fact, Amma accepts no responsibility but simply attributes all such happenings to God and the power of the faith of the individuals.

And so, too, it is with what Kṛṣṇa calls *arthārthis*. These people come to Amma not seeking rescue from peril, but for help in fulfilling their material desires. "Amma, help me get into graduate school!" "Amma, please help my business be successful!" "Amma, please help me get my visa!" "Please help me get my book published!" The arthārthis see Amma as a conduit of grace and always share their desires with her. Here, too, we often see these people coming back the next week, month or year, beaming with a smile, and thanking Amma for fulfilling their prayers.

How is all this possible? If we look to the Vedas, we see that they emphatically recommend approaching a mahātma for fulfilling one's desires.

> yaṁ yaṁ lokaṁ manasā saṁvibhāti
> viśuddha-sattvaḥ kāmayate yāṁśca kāmān |
> taṁ taṁ lokaṁ jayate tāṁśca kāmāṁ-

stasmād-ātma-jñāṁ hyarcayedbhūti-kāmaḥ ||

"The man of pure mind wins those worlds that he mentally wishes for and those enjoyable things that he desires. Therefore one desirous of prosperity should worship the knower of the Self."

[Muṇḍaka Upaniṣad, 3.1.10]

The idea is that a mahātma can obtain anything he 'desires' through the power of his *saṅkalpa* [willful resolve]. However when the scriptures refer to 'purity of mind,' they mean a mind cleansed of all desires. The implication is that, having no desires of his own, a mahātma gladly takes up the desires of those who petition him and blesses them accordingly.

That does not mean that everyone has their desires fulfilled. To some extent, *prārabdha karma* [fate based on prior actions] plays a role in this process. But Amma is a mother, and what mother doesn't want her children to be happy? If you ask her for something you desire, and it doesn't hurt anyone and it falls in line with *dharma* [righteousness], definitely she will do her utmost to help you—either through the reach of her humanitarian projects or through her advice or through the power of her resolve.

Some people may think it incorrect to come to Amma for such worldly things, but in the Gīta, Kṛṣṇa refers to both the ārtas and the arthārthis as 'noble' and says the very fact they are turning to God for relief and material fulfillment shows that they have performed innumerable good actions in this or past lives. However such devotion has its limitations, and the scriptures tell us that while it is fine to begin our life with such a mentality, we should not allow it to end there. Such devotion is not very stable. When the prayers of such people are not answered, they rarely come back. And even when such people get what they came for, they often go back to their regular lives, forgetting about Amma (until the next problem comes, that is). We should try to evolve—to seek from Amma the more precious treasures she has to offer.

This brings us to the next group of people who come to see Amma, the *jijñāsus*—the seekers of knowledge. The jijñāsu is a devotee of a different caliber. He understands that even if his problems are remedied, more problems will come. Furthermore he understands the limitations of worldly attainments. He sees Amma as a *sadguru*—an enlightened master who can serve as a means to not temporary but permanent peace and happiness.

In fact, the scriptures tell us that everyone's devotion begins as that of an ārta, then evolves into that of an arthārthi and only then evolves into that of a jijñāsu[1]. These stages represent an evolution in understanding and focus of the devotee. Some people have progressed through this evolution in previous births and begin their relationship with Amma as a seeker of Truth. Others go through the evolution in this birth alone. Others will still require future births.

If we investigate, we see that some people come to Amma seeking a material objective, but come away from their very first *darśan* seeking the supreme. This is due to a *samskāra*—a latent inclination carried over from past lives for spiritual life. This samskāra has been waiting there, just below the surface of the conscious mind, for the touch, words or look of a mahātma to awaken it. It sounds rather mystical, but we can find the same phenomenon in many areas of life, not only in spirituality. Many great writers, musicians, athletes and scientists show no predilection for their respective fields until that passion is suddenly ignited through a certain novel or concert or coach, etc. Thereafter, no one can deter them.

When I first came to see Amma, I was not interested in spirituality. As I was raised in an orthodox Brahmin community, I was

---

[1] It is said that it is better to be an *arthārthi* than an *ārta* because the arthārthi seeks God whenever he desires something, i.e. quite often, and the ārta only thinks about God when he is in a pinch.

'religious.' I did *sandhyā-vandanam*[2] and other orthodox Hindu observances. But I considered such practices only as a means to fulfill my material desires. I had wanted to become a doctor but had missed being admitted into medical school by a very narrow margin. Abandoning this dream, I had recently taken employment with a bank, and they had placed me in a branch in a small town called Harippād. I was very irritated about this because not only was I not in medical school, but I also had to work in a tiny place where, at that time, there were no proper restaurants!

What I wanted more than anything was to be transferred to another branch of the bank—somewhere in a city. When I heard about Amma (whose *āśram* is located about 16 miles south of Harippād), I thought that perhaps she could work some of her magic and get me transferred. So, one day I took a bus to Parayakaḍavu and went for Amma's darśan.

When I arrived Amma was in Kṛṣṇa Bhāva[3]. The family temple where Amma conducted the darśan was right next to the cowshed. Seeing Amma dressed as Lord Kṛṣṇa, I was not sure what was going on. However I felt very peaceful. When I came for Amma's darśan, before I could even say anything, Amma said, "Oh, you have a problem with work." She then handed me a large handful of small red flowers and told me to offer 48 of them on Devi's head when Amma came out in Devi Bhāva[4] later that night. (To my surprise when I counted the flowers Amma had handed me, there were *exactly* 48.)

Back in those days, when Amma would come out in Devi Bhāva, she would first dance in front of the temple. So when Amma was dancing, I offered the flowers as instructed. After

---

[2] A ritualistic series of prayers and prostrations performed at sunset and sunrise.

[3] A special form of *darśan*, wherein Amma took upon the attire and manner of Śrī Kṛṣṇa.

[4] Amma giving *darśan* in the attire and manner of the Divine Mother of the Universe

the dance was complete, I joined the queue for Amma's Devi darśan. This time when Amma held me, I began to cry. I was very touched by Amma's love, compassion and kindness. Amma told me to sit by the side of her chair. I did so, at which point she spontaneously initiated me into a *mantra*. After a while Amma asked me to meditate for some time. I told Amma that I had never practiced meditation before. She told me it would be enough for me to just close my eyes. So I decided to try.

After what I thought had been about 10 minutes, I opened my eyes, thinking that other people may like to sit next to Amma. When I did so, none of the people who were previously sitting around me were there. I looked at my watch. It showed that two hours had passed! I thought this could not be correct, that my watch must be wrong. So I asked the man sitting at my side what time it was. He confirmed it; I had been meditating for two hours. Confused, I got up, offered my *praṇām* [prostration] to Amma and returned to Harippād.

The next day, I simply could not go to work. I felt intoxicated, drifting on a cloud of peace and happiness. I was afraid that if I went to work—where my primary job was counting money—it would be disastrous. So I called in sick and didn't even leave the house. The only thoughts in my mind were of Amma and the soothing peace of her darśan. The next day, I again called in sick. It was only on the third day that I decided I had to go back and see Amma. After that, I just called in sick for the rest of the week, and spent as much time as I could with her. My whole focus had changed. Amma had triggered the beginnings of a spiritual inclination within me. This was not the case only for me. Many of Amma's disciples who are now the senior *swāmis* [monks] initially came to Amma with some material desire, but soon found themselves seeking the supreme.

Sometimes this shift comes quickly, sometimes it takes time. For some the samskāra may not be so deep, but they become quite attached to Amma nonetheless—to the warmth of her affection and attention, to her kindness and darśan, etc. These people return to see Amma whenever possible, and slowly their relationship with her grows deeper. They begin trying to put Amma's teachings into practice. Perhaps they get initiated into a mantra by Amma or at Amma's encouragement begin participating in some selfless-service projects of the Āśram. As their minds become more and more purified and their spiritual understanding deepens, their focus gradually shifts. Gradually they find themselves more interested in spiritual goals than worldly ones.

Sometimes, this change of perspective even comes through receiving Amma's material blessings. There was a devotee from America who had written a novel and was burning to get it published. He brought the manuscript to Amma, and Amma smiled at him and reverently touched the book to her forehead. A few weeks later, he secured a book deal with a major publisher. The devotee was ecstatic. Before he knew it, his book was on the shelves of bookstores throughout the country. But it wasn't long before he realized that, despite being a published author, he still felt incomplete. Upon reflecting, he realized that even if Amma were to fulfill his every wish, this feeling would remain. He clearly saw the reality that only through realizing the Self would he feel the peace and contentment for which he was longing.

Amma herself is the greatest inspiration for following the spiritual path. We see the peace, happiness and contentment that clearly radiate from her and are mystified. Here is someone who works 24 hours a day, draws no salary, has no possessions, wears only simple clothes and yet is infinitely happier than any creatively productive, financially rich and physically robust person in the world. Observing Amma, we quickly realize that she must know a secret regarding happiness that we have yet to learn. Confronted with this, we soon find oursleves more interested in learning this secret than attaining finite material gains.

In Bṛhadāraṇyaka Upaniṣad, we are presented with a scenario wherein the wife of a *ṛṣi* [sage] has caught on to the fact that her husband possesses such knowledge and refuses to settle for anything less than discipleship. The ṛṣi's name is Yājñavalkya, and the wife's name is Maitreyi. Yājñavalkya has a second wife, Kātyāyani, as well. Of these two, Maitreyi is quite spiritually inclined, whereas Kātyāyani is materialistic. One day Yājñavalkya informs Maitreyi that he is going to take *sannyāsa* [renunciation] and thus end his relationship with her and Kātyāyani. When he begins explaining how he is going to divide his property between the two women, Maitreyi suddenly speaks up and says, "Sir, if I had all the money in the whole wide world, would it make me immortal[5]?" Yājñavalkya says that it would not. Hearing this, Maitreyi boldly tells him that if it cannot make her immortal then it is of no value to her. Knowing that her husband is a storehouse of spiritual wisdom, Maitreyi says, "I am only interested in your knowledge. Tell me what you know." Maitreyi had real *jijñāsa* [thirst for knowledge]. She understood the true value of a sadguru and did not want to squander the precious opportunity before her.

Some of the people who come to see Amma were thirsting for Self-knowledge even before meeting Amma. Understanding a sadguru is essential for any serious seeker, they come to Amma with the intention of seeking her guidance. Such people find in Amma a veritable spiritual cure-all. Through her they find avenues for engaging in selfless service, are given meditation techniques, are initiated into mantras and are given the opportunity to forge a deep bond with a living spiritual master who turns no one away regardless of their spiritual qualifications. Furthermore, through Amma's talks and books, she helps clear the path to the ultimate goal of life—removing the sundry confusions and misconceptions about spirituality that are all too prevalent in today's 'Information Age.' Such people leave their first meeting with Amma feeling like they've truly hit the spiritual jackpot.

[5] By the word 'immortal,' eternal happiness is indicated.

Many such seekers are relatively new to spiritual life, but others have been plying the spiritual path for decades—*sannyāsis*, Buddhist and Christian monks, etc. They come to Amma with the hopes of receiving Amma's blessings and attaining deeper insight. And in Amma's presence—through the powerful, pure vibration created by Amma—they indeed experience deeper levels of clarity than previously known to them. Furthermore, spending time with Amma, such people receive immense inspiration, as in Amma they finally come face-to-face with someone who clearly has attained the goal to which they have dedicated their lives. This helps them to continue forward on the path with more enthusiasm and vigor.

Many years ago a senior sannyāsi from a well-known spiritual organization came to Amma's āśram. I remember watching him before he entered Amma's room. Right or wrong, I thought that something about him seemed a little puffed up. But when he left a few hours later, I saw the traces of tears in his eyes. I asked him how his meeting with Amma had been. He responded, "Today I feel as if my lifetime of spiritual pursuit has finally taken wing."

In fact there is another group of people who come to see Amma—cynics. These people think, "Something's fishy here! There's no way this lady can really be so selfless and compassionate! I'm going to go there and blow the lid off the whole thing!" Such people have always come to see Amma. If their hearts are closed, they stand around rolling their eyes for a while and then leave. But if there is even a small space inside them that is open, Amma will find it and plant a seed that will soon sprout. It was like this with one of Amma's senior *brahmacāris*. He was a student at a prestigious film school in Pune. During his college years he had become friendly with a Communist student group and, as such, was dead set against religion, spirituality and particularly 'living saints.' When his family encouraged him to visit Amma's āśram, he readily agreed, thinking that he would use the opportunity to do research toward making a film about 'phony saints.' However, as he stood watching Amma with his filmmaker's eye, Amma's eye found him. He could not help but see how Amma was sacrificing her rest and comfort in order to bring light and love into the lives of others. Soon he found himself her disciple.

Although on the surface these groups of people seem to be coming for different reasons, Amma says in truth everyone—not only those who come to see Amma, but everyone in the world—is seeking the same thing: to experience the fullness of the Self. Amma says that it is this longing that is driving us forward in life. It is the motivation behind our friendships, the motivation behind our marriages, our divorces, our having children, our pursuing and changing careers, our buying houses, cars, going to movies... All are striving for the same thing. But the fullness for which we are looking—both the spiritual aspirant and the materialist—is not a finite thing. It is infinite—as expansive as the entire universe. And no one can attain infinity from tallying up a list of finite things. Even 20 trillion multiplied by 20 trillion results in a finite number. As long as we seek this happiness through the material world, we will never attain the fullness we are seeking.

If you are reading this book you probably have at least some level of *jijñāsa* [thirst for spiritual knowledge], otherwise you would be reading something else. But all of us should reflect on how much of us is a jijñāsu [seeker of Truth]. If we introspect, we will see that we all move back and forth between the three types of devotion discussed in this chapter. There are times when we are sincere seekers and there are times when our focus becomes more materialistic. The more we attune ourselves with Amma, the more we find the quest for spiritual knowledge becoming our prime volition. Whatever our level of devotion, Amma accepts all unconditionally. This is part of her greatness. Knowing that in most of us jijñāsa is not fully ignited, Amma encourages us to share our fears and desires with her—to come to her with our ārta and arthārthi devotion. In this way, she can enter every aspect of our lives and, thereby, help us all the more in our spiritual evolution. With our effort and Amma's grace, our devotion can even transcend jijñāsa to reach the pinnacle of devotion, *jñāna*—a knowledge wherein we understand that everything within and without is divine.

Chapter Two:

The Bond That Destroys All Bonds

"The relationship between a sadguru and disciple is incomparable—there is nothing like it. It has a permanent effect on the disciple. In that relationship the disciple can never come to any harm."

—Amma

THE RELATIONSHIP ONE DEVELOPS with a *sadguru*, an enlightened spiritual master, is unlike any other. This is because it is the only type of relationship wherein one person gives everything and the other only takes. Perhaps the mother-child relationship is the most comparable.

Here is an incident that recently took place in Amṛtapuri that demonstrates this principle. Amma was giving *darśan* to a huge crowd. In fact, all week long the darśans had been like this—lasting into the wee hours of the morning, only to repeat the process again a few hours later. Witnessing this, an Indian devotee from America approached Amma. He said, "Amma, why can't you take a vacation? Perhaps you could go to Hawaii and relax on the beach. We devotees would pay for it, and you could rest your body for a week or so."

Amma laughed at the man's suggestion and gave him a compassionate smile. She then said, "Don't you have a son? If he were sick or sad or needed you, would you be able to just take off and go to the beach? Of course not. You would stay with him, console him and help him feel better. This is how it is with Amma. All are my children, and I cannot leave them to take some vacation."

So a sadguru like Amma really is an *amma*—a 'mother'—in terms of her love and compassion and desire to raise her disciples. But there is a difference—because a regular mother gains tremendous joy from her child and the experience of being a mother, whereas a sadguru is full and complete with or without his disciples. Furthermore, in a relationship with a sadguru, one can have complete faith and trust, for not only does he love the disciple unconditionally, but his understanding regarding the disciple's past, present and future is so clear that he can guide him with an otherwise impossible insight. Our biological mother may love us, but her vision is limited and her advice is often biased due to her over-attachment.

We can also see such limitations in relationships with therapists or psychologists. There is one young devotee in America who is a big fan of heavy-metal rock music. A few years ago during one of Amma's summer tours, he told me about a documentary he had recently seen about one of his favorite heavy-metal bands. It seems at one point the relationships between the band members had become so poor that they decided to hire a therapist to help repair them. The band was also suffering from feelings of creative stagnation. The film documented the band's therapy sessions to overcome these problems. The devotee explained to me that when he was watching the film, there was one very specific moment when he saw a startling difference between a psychologist's therapy and the type of help Amma provides. The point was toward the end of the film when the band told the therapist that they felt they no longer required his services. The devotee told me that the reaction of the therapist—whom the band was paying $40,000 per month to keep on call—said it all. The therapist had become completely dependent on the band—dependent on their monthly checks, dependent on the name and fame coming to him through the work, dependent on the whole set-up. The band no longer needed the therapist, but the therapist now needed the band.

The bond we form with Amma is not like this. It is unique in that it is a bond that frees us from all bonds. It is a dependency that leads to total independence. I can unequivocally say that, more than anything else, it has been my bond with Amma that has kept me focused in spiritual life. The *guru*-disciple relationship is the true source of support and strength for a seeker.

Soon after I met Amma, she became my sole focus. I immediately wanted to resign my post at the bank where I was employed. However, Amma told me that I should continue to work for a few more years. She advised me to see all the people who came there as sent to me by Amma herself. In this way, my work itself would become a spiritual practice. Other than that, Amma did not mandate any spiritual practices. I would come to the āśram in the evenings and spend weekends there as well. At that time, things around Amma were very loose. Other than the *bhāva darśans*, which took place on Sundays, Tuesdays and Thursdays, there were no fixed timings for seeing Amma. People would just come as they pleased. Back then, the other youths and I (who eventually became Amma's first monastic disciples) basically just 'hung out' with Amma. More than 'spirituality,' we were interested in *Amma*—in her motherly love and affection. And Amma didn't seem interested in pushing us into spiritual practices either. Amma had initiated us all into *mantras* and taught us how to meditate, so we engaged in those practices for some time each day. But nothing was regimented, like a discipline. Other than that we just did what Amma did. If she sat in meditation, we would try to meditate along with her. When she sang *bhajans*, which was at the least every sundown, we would join her. That was it.

Amma would play village games with young children, such as *kabaḍi* and *kottu kallu kaḷi*, and we would sit and watch—laughing and enjoying the beauty and purity of Amma's interactions with the children. Occasionally we might ask some spiritual questions but, to be honest, most of us were not that interested. Amma would tell us about various things she had done the previous day, things that had happened in the village, perhaps stories about visiting the homes of various devotees. It was not a guru-disciple relationship. It was more like a friendship or the relationship between a mother and her children. We would talk very freely with Amma, even argue with her. We had no idea about the proper ways of conducting oneself around a spiritual master. If Amma would do some chores, we would assist her. If she did some cooking, we would help her cook. When the devotees came to talk with Amma, we would sit around and listen.

At the time we did not realize what was happening. We simply did as we pleased. But, as always, Amma was functioning at the highest level of understanding and awareness. Amma *loves*, but her love is very intelligent. If she had disciplined us from the beginning, many of us would have bolted for the door! She was secretly binding us to her with the unbreakable silk thread of her love.

When we tell stories like this about the old days, many devotees all but swoon at the thought of such a life with Amma. It's true; it was a golden and magical time. I would be lying if I told you otherwise. However, there is no need to be sad, thinking that what was available then is not available today. True, the number of people coming to see Amma is much larger now, but if you look at what Amma is doing at her programs, it is the exact same things she was doing way back then with us. Just as we would sit around and watch Amma play games with the children, today devotees watch Amma as she holds up the infants who are brought for darśan—the way she nibbles on their cheeks and gums their toes. Just as we would talk to Amma about various mundane things, so too Amma still engages people coming for darśan and sitting around her in various light conversation, perhaps telling them about places she has given programs and things that have happened there. And during Amma's programs, what does everyone do? When Amma meditates, they meditate; when Amma sings bhajans, they sing bhajans. And when Amma occasionally engages in various cleaning chores—either in the *āśram* or at the end of Devi Bhāva—everyone joins in, just like we did long ago. So, other than the number of people coming, nothing has really changed. Furthermore, even though we have less one-on-one interaction with Amma, somehow Amma's *saṅkalpa* [resolve] adjusts for this. If we are open, our bond with her will become just as firm as it would were Amma to have more time to spend with each of us individually.

Of course Amma's darśan is central to the deepening of our bond with Amma. In Amma's arms, we feel completely unburdened. In the peace of that embrace, we feel an undeniable sense of oneness with Amma. In fact, Amma's darśan makes an incredible impact on people because it verily gives them a taste of God—a taste of their True Self. For many this is an eye-opening experience that reshuffles their priorities in life. It is as if the pin that served as the axis for one's world becomes removed and set anew.

Ostensibly, it is a strange thing—allowing a total stranger to embrace you. But no one has reluctance or feelings of shyness or awkwardness when first approaching Amma for darśan. It is as if they are hugging their mother—or even their very own Self. One leaves, feeling that they have known Amma all their life. That is because the first darśan is the beginning of a beginningless relationship.

A minute spent watching Amma is never wasted. We can learn many spiritual principles through watching and contemplating upon her actions. In fact we learn much more through someone's example than we do through their words. If a father tells his son not to smoke yet smokes himself, it will not make much impact. His actions speak much louder than his words. So too, when we spend time watching Amma interact with people, we find that we naturally begin imbibing some of her qualities—be they external or internal. It is as Amma says, "If you visit a perfume factory, the fragrance will cling to your body."

In fact this is one of the principles behind meditation focused on a specific form of God. When one concentrates on a form of a God, one naturally begins to acquire that form's qualities. We meditate on the Divine Mother and our mind is filled with thoughts of love and compassion. If we meditate on Hanumān and think of his strength and bravery, we will gain in mental strength and courage. Meditation on the form of Lord Śiva, the epitome of detachment and austerity, will help us gain in detachment and become more steadfast in our spiritual practices.

This is not a mystical process. The same thing happens all the time in regular life. Take the example of someone who becomes obsessed with a given movie star or musician. Don't they often begin walking like them, dressing like them and talking like them? In 2001, I remember suddenly seeing dozens of boys sporting sideburns and soul patches. It seemed to come out of nowhere. In fact some of the boys were not even old enough to properly grow them, yet they were trying their utmost nonetheless. When I inquired about the trend, someone told me that there was a new hit Bollywood film called *Dil Chahta Hai*, in which the star sported such a hairstyle and facial hair. If simply watching a movie once or twice can create such a strong sense of identification, imagine the transformation possible through an intense meditation practice conducted on a daily basis? Watching Amma as she gives darśan, as she sings bhajans, as she gives talks, etc., is actually a form of meditation—open-eyed meditation. And in the same way that one imbibes the characteristics and qualities of one's beloved deity through closed-eye meditation, one begins picking up Amma's qualities through focusing on her and associating with her. Witnessing Amma's compassion, we desire to become more compassionate. Seeing her patience and simplicity, we strive to become more patient and simple as well.

Amma says, "We come to understand what truth, *dharma*, selflessness and love are because the guru *lives* those qualities.

The guru is the life of those qualities. By obeying and emulating the sadguru, we cultivate those qualities in ourselves."

Let me give you an example of how this imbibing takes place. In Amṛtapuri, Amma if she is not still giving darśan comes to the bhajan hall every night just before 7:00 to lead the devotional singing. When Amma arrives, there is usually a dozen or so small children lined up behind her *pīṭham* [guru's seat], all jostling for the spot closest to where Amma will sit. For the *āśramites* and devotees, it can be quite an endearing thing to witness. In August of 2008, there was a three-year-old Indian boy from America visiting the āśram. He was there with all the other kids, trying to get a good spot. And then, just before Amma walked onto the dais, he simply stood atop Amma's pīṭham. Of course all eyes were on him. He then offered his *pranams* by pressing his hands together over his head in the *añjali mudra*, just as Amma does, and then sat down cross-legged, just like Amma. He then grabbed one of Amma's drumsticks and began whacking Amma's mike-stand to a rhythm, just like Amma sometimes does during the bhajans. When Amma saw him sitting there, she just started laughing. Someone removed him, but after Amma sat down she called the boy back to sit at her side. She gave him the mike. Immediately the boy began trying to say *prema-svarūpikaḷum ātma-svarūpikaḷumāya ellāvarkkum namaskāram*—"I bow down to everyone whose nature is divine love and the Self"—which is what Amma says every time she begins a public talk. Then he started singing his bhajan set with a song to Lord Gaṇeśa, just like Amma does. It was very cute to watch. Like most three-year-olds, his pronunciation was not all that clear, but the feeling was pure Amma. All the devotees and āśramites kept the beat for the child as he sang away. You can say that it is just a child and meaningless, but it is a perfect example of how we absorb Amma's mannerisms, actions and qualities. They become our habits, and habit becomes character. If we are even somewhat mature, we will start to inculcate Amma's qualities on deeper levels—the love, compassion and selflessness that are the driving force behind her every word and action.

So although this phase of our relationship wherein we simply sit around watching Amma may seem on the surface to be something rather inconsequential, it is in fact a crucial element in building our bond. Only when our bond with the guru is deep and firm, will we have the faith and trust required to properly follow the guru's advice, instructions and teachings.

If we read the epic Mahābhārata, we will see that it is not until the middle of the book that Arjuna becomes Kṛṣṇa's disciple. Before that, just like with Amma, it is more a relationship between friends. In fact, in the fourth chapter of the Bhagavad-Gīta, Kṛṣṇa addresses Arjuna not only as a devotee, but also as *sakhe*—friend. The trust, openness and heartfelt closeness of true friendship is essential for a fruitful guru-disciple relationship.

In the scriptures, attachment is constantly decried as a serious obstacle to spiritual progress. Amma herself often speaks about the importance of transcending our likes and dislikes and dependencies. Therefore, when we find ourselves becoming attached to Amma, it is only natural that it might create some confusion. Along these lines I remember an incident that took place back in the mid-1980s. Back then, Amma would almost always attend our morning meditation sessions. When the meditation was over, she would answer any questions we might have. On one such morning one of the *brahmacāris*—now Swāmi Amṛtagītānanda—was having this very same doubt. In fact he did not mention this doubt to Amma but it had been plaguing him throughout his meditation. He had been thinking, "I have come here to transcend all my attachments, yet I am becoming so attached to Amma! Isn't this just another form of bondage? Have I not just jumped from one form of *māya* [illusion] into another?"

Suddenly Amma looked directly at him and said, "Attachment to one's guru and the āśram is not bondage or māya. All other attachments are bondage. A thorn is used to remove other thorns. So, also, attachment to the guru leads one to liberation."

Similarly, a few years ago a new brahmacāri was standing near Amma as she gave darśan. Suddenly Amma looked up at him with a loving smile. She called him to her side and asked him what he was thinking. He said, "I am becoming so attached to Amma, but I worry in the end it is only going to cause me pain." Amma said, "That attachment is the attachment that destroys all other attachments. Even if it brings you pain, that pain will purify you. It will become a path to God."

Amma is the most available person in the world. To see her, all one needs to do is come and join the queue. There are no obstacles. She is constantly extending her hand in order to pull us up, but it is up to us to grab Amma's hand. Once we do so, she will hold on tight until we can walk on our own. That is not to say the bond one develops with Amma is only for beginners. It will continually mature and deepen throughout our lives. As we grow, it becomes more and more central to who we are—an essential aspect of our existence. In fact the final attainment is the knowledge that guru and disciple have always been one—the ultimate bond. But in the beginning the external bond is the focus. It is this bond and the precious memories that we gain spending time around Amma that will carry us through the difficult periods of life, which come to one and all. Eventually, when we are ready, there will be a shift in our relationship with Amma. Then the disciplining begins. For us, the first batch of brahmacāris, that shift took place after two or three years. One day the mother becomes the guru.

Chapter Three:

The Importance of the Guru

"The light of the guru's grace helps us to see and remove the obstacles in our path."

—Amma

AMMA SAYS THAT THE GURU appears only when there is a disciple. This means that until we are ready, Amma's *guru bhāva* [guruhood] will remain unmanifest for us. Conversely, the moment we are ready, it will be there waiting. We find the same thing in the Mahābhārata. Throughout the first half of the epic, Kṛṣṇa never acts as a guru to Arjuna. This is because Arjuna, the disciple, has yet to take birth. But when Arjuna admits his inability to solve his problems for himself and surrenders in a puddle at Kṛṣṇa's feet, begging for his instruction and guidance, Kṛṣṇa, the guru, is immediately there saying, "You grieve for those who should not be grieved for," etc. It is only at this point that the actual teaching of the Gīta begins.

We speak of Amma's 'guru bhāva,' but in fact every face of Amma is a *bhāva* [an assumed mood]. Unlike us, Amma does not identify with the various costumes she wears in the world. We may claim that we are a 'teacher' or a 'student,' a 'businessman' or a 'doctor' or an 'artist,' etc., but Amma's only identification is with the True Self—the blissful consciousness that serves as the substratum to thought and the physical universe. So, Amma is not inherently a guru. Neither is she inherently a 'mother,' a 'humanitarian' or any other such thing. She knows that, inherently, she is eternal, blissful consciousness alone. Out of her compassion,

Amma takes the bhāva of a mother, humanitarian, friend, God or guru, whenever it is required. The child, needing love and comfort, invokes the mother. The suffering poor invoke the humanitarian. The one seeking a heartfelt companion invokes the friend. The devotee invokes God. The disciple invokes the guru. (Only when we understand this, we will see the full significance of seemingly flippant statements Amma makes such as, "They call me 'Mother' and because of that I call them 'children.' Amma does not know any more than that.") Ultimately all such divisions are based on ignorance. In the pinnacle of spiritual wisdom in which Amma abides, there is only unity—disciple and guru, devotee and God, child and mother... all are eternally one. This is why Amma says, "For there to be a guru, there must first be a disciple."

A few years ago Amma was being interviewed for an American television documentary. The documentary would present the views of a dozen or so leaders from the world's major religions. Amma was the sole representative for Hinduism. At the end of the two-hour-long interview, the directors asked Amma to introduce herself to the camera. They explained that they wanted Amma to simply look into the camera and say something to the effect of "Hello, my name is Śrī Māta Amṛtānandamayi Devi, and I am a Hindu spiritual leader and humanitarian from Kerala, India." After they explained this, the other *swāmis* and I all wondered what Amma would do, because this is simply not something that Amma says. In the past 30 years, I have never heard Amma make a statement like that. So we all wondered what would happen. Well, Amma smiled but declined. We thought that would be the end of it, but the directors persisted. They said something to the effect of "Come on, Amma, all the other spiritual leaders did it." But, still, Amma wasn't budging. If there is one thing that Amma always is, it is natural. For example, she will never pose for a photograph. And for Amma to say a sentence like this simply wasn't natural. But due to her compassion, Amma did not want to hurt the documentarians' feelings. We thought the whole thing was over, and then suddenly Amma said, "This visible form people call 'Amma' or 'Māta Amṛtānandamayi Devi,' but the indwelling Self has no name or address. It is all-pervading." From this statement, we see that the guru bhāva is something that Amma dons only when the disciple invokes it. It is a response to a need. When the need matures it appears. But Amma's true nature has no name or address. It is beyond everything.

THERE ARE TWO MAIN FACETS to Amma's guru bhāva: knowledge and discipline. With regards to receiving knowledge, some people think a guru is not necessary. They believe that it is enough to follow the scriptures. But the scriptures themselves repeatedly state that a guru is essential if one hopes to reach the final goal. Ādi Śaṅkarācārya[1] writes in his commentary on Muṇḍaka Upaniṣad that even if one is schooled in Sanskrit, systematic logic and other such *śāstras* [sciences], he should not attempt to attain Self-knowledge without a guru.

Why is the guru so essential? Amma says, "People who undertake a journey with the help of a map may nevertheless lose their way and wander about. Also a map will not inform you about the presence of highwaymen or wild animals. Only if we have an experienced guide can we travel without any tension. If there is somebody with you who is familiar with the way, the journey will be smooth and easy."

In all fields of life—whether it be science, art or business—a teacher is required. It is no different with spirituality. In fact, spirituality is the most subtle area of knowledge because one is actually studying his own Self. In biology, the scientist uses a microscope to study microbes. In chemistry, it is chemicals. In spirituality, the scientist himself, as it were, is the very subject. Thus, the subject is outside the scope of our primary means of knowledge—the senses and intellect. With the subject being so

[1] The commentaries and texts of Ādi Śaṅkarācārya (circa 800 CE) consolidated the Advaita Vedānta school of thought.

subtle, a teacher is needed all the more. As Amma often says, "A teacher is needed even to learn to tie one's shoes!" A sadguru like Amma not only explains the spiritual path to us and clears the doubts we face along the way but, also, through their keen insight into our character, assists us in transcending the obstacles we confront along the way.

In fact, Amma is always providing knowledge—be it a deeper insight into *dharma*, *karma yoga*, meditation or the ultimate truth. A ceaseless river of knowledge flows from Amma's lips. She is ever ready to guide people toward more intelligent, harmonious ways of living and thinking. In Amṛtapuri, she holds question-and-answer sessions with the residents and visitors once a week, and similar sessions are conducted during Amma's World Tour retreats. To invoke this aspect of Amma's guru bhāva, all one needs is an interest.[2] This shows that when Amma says that "the guru in Amma will only appear when there is a disciple," she is primarily speaking about the guru as a disciplinarian.

The final goal of spiritual life is, in theory, very simple: complete assimilation of the knowledge that our true nature is not the body, emotions or intellect, but all-expansive, eternal, blissful consciousness. When we wake in the morning, we need not open our eyes and look in a mirror in order to know who we are. There is no doubt: "Who am I? Am I a man? A woman? A donkey? Indian? American? Japanese?" We simply *know*. Spiritual knowledge has to be assimilated to the same level of conviction. In fact it is a rather odd thing: *through* the mind, we have to come to understand that we are *not* the mind. The mind is the source of ignorance and, at the same time, the means to liberation. As Śaṅkarācārya writes:

> vāyunā'nīyate meghaḥ punastenaiva nīyate |
> manasā kalpyate bandho mokṣastenaiva kalpyate ||

[2] The more genuine our interest, the more in-depth Amma's answer

"Clouds are brought in by the wind and again driven away by the same agency. Similarly, man's bondage is caused by the mind, and liberation too is caused by that alone." [Vivekacuḍāmaṇi, 172]

In essence, intellectually grasping the concept that one's nature is consciousness is not very difficult. However, for lifetimes we have been thinking in the exact opposite line, completely identifying with the body, emotions and intellect and associating our happiness solely with the fulfillment of our desires. Such thinking has become so habitual that we cannot reverse it so easily. To explain this phenomenon, Amma likes to give the example of a man who, after years of carrying his wallet in his pants pocket, one day decides to start carrying it in his breast pocket. If you ask him, when he is relaxed and has time to think, where he keeps his wallet, he may tell you, "Oh, I keep it in my breast pocket now." However, when he is in a hurry to pay for his coffee, he reaches into the pocket in his pants. What is technically his knowledge and what is his actual behavior are polar opposites.

Once there was a homeless man who neither had a job nor a place to stay. He survived only by eating whatever he could, often having no choice but to dig through dumpsters and trashcans. Then one day he was approached by a humanitarian. The humanitarian was selecting homeless people to rehabilitate. The man was given lodging and a stipend for food. He was also given money for a college education. The man was overjoyed at the compassion of the philanthropist. He thanked him heartily, enrolled in school and completely turned his life around. Ten years later, he had graduated with an MBA and owned a company listed in the Fortune 500. One day he was riding in the back of his limo, smoking a fine Cuban cigar, watching the city roll by through his tinted windows, when suddenly he started shouting at the chauffer. "Stop! Stop! For God's sake, stop the car! What are you? Insane?"

The chauffer slammed on the breaks. "What? What is it, sir?"

The homeless-man-turned-business-tycoon shot back, "What is it? You didn't see? The man on the corner just threw away a perfectly good slice of pizza!"

The man now had enough money to buy 100 Pizza Huts, yet such understanding had not thoroughly saturated his subconscious mind. Seeing the pizza being tossed into the bin, he forgot his current status and his old thinking patterns came to the fore.

Just about anyone can enroll in a 'Philosophies of Eastern Religion 101' class and come away with a basic understanding of the Vedānta philosophy. However, such people do not attain enlightenment. The reason lies in their minds. Their minds have not been sufficiently purified to properly assimilate the knowledge. For most of us, our mind lacks discriminative thinking, subtlety, awareness, patience and focus. It is also full of egoistic notions and is constantly plagued by likes and dislikes. For one to truly assimilate spiritual knowledge, all these impurities must go. In many regards, achieving mental purity is much more difficult than attaining knowledge. It is even said that once mental purity is attained, liberation is but a matter of course. It is in regards to helping the disciple attain this mental purity that the guru as disciplinarian comes in.

"As long as you haven't mastered your mind, you need to abide by certain rules and restraints according to the guru's instructions," Amma says. "Once you have mastered your mind, there is nothing to fear."

THE FOUR QUALIFICATIONS

The scriptures specify several areas in which we must discipline and purify the mind. Only after we have accomplished this, can spiritual knowledge be properly assimilated. In Sanskrit these areas are collectively referred to as *sādhana catuṣṭaya sampatti*—the four-fold qualifications[3]. These include: *viveka, vairāgya, mumukṣutvam* and *śamādi ṣatka sampatti*—discrimination, dispassion, thirst for liberation and the six-fold disciplines beginning with mind-control.

So, in some ways, a sadguru like Amma is like a coach—not only teaching us the rules of life, but also making sure we are adequately fit to play the game. Like any good coach, Amma knows the mental strengths and weaknesses of all of her players. She also knows how to help them overcome those weaknesses—by hook or crook. Through personal instruction, creating challenging situations, correcting mistakes and helping the disciple to see his weaknesses for himself, Amma helps us to strengthen and refine our mind until it is capable of assimilating the ultimate truth. In fact, if the disciple's mind is completely purified, it is said his assimilation of the Truth will take place the moment it is first explained to him—the so-called 'instant realization.'

VIVEKA, VAIRĀGYA & MUMUKṢUTVAM

The first area of mental refinement is viveka. In its ultimate sense, viveka means the ability to discriminate between *ātma* and *anātma*—the Self and the non-Self. Both when looking within and when looking at the external world, one should be able to separate reality from non-reality—the wheat from the chaff, so to speak. The need for this constant dichotomizing is one of the reasons why spiritual life is said to be like 'walking a razor's edge[4].' But we can also apply this discrimination on a more relative level as well. Ultimately, life is a series of decisions. In every moment, in every interaction, with every breath, we have the choice to act,

[3] They are referred to as 'qualifications' because Self-knowledge will take root only in a mind in which these qualities have been properly developed. If we are deficient in any of these, it means that we need to put in more effort to develop them, not that we are unqualified for spiritual life.

[4] Kaṭha Upaniṣad, 1.3.14

speak and think, either in a line that will bring us closer to our goal or away from it. So, viveka is acting in accordance with the firm understanding that the goal of human life—permanent happiness—can never come from impermanent things. It can only come from something eternal.

Once we understand the difference between what brings temporary happiness and what brings eternal happiness, we will naturally begin moving away from the former and toward the latter. The impulse to move away from transient happiness is called vairāgya, and the impulse to move toward permanent happiness is called mumukṣutvam. In this way, vairāgya, mumukṣutvam and viveka are all directly related.

Mumukṣutvam [thirst for liberation] in fact is inherent. Everyone desires transcendence. No one wants any limits placed upon their happiness. Whenever we feel frustrated with our limitations, it is a reflection of our inherent mumukṣutvam. But most people fail to understand that feelings of limitation cannot be avoided as long as we set our sights on limited things—i.e. sense pleasures, relationships, attainments, etc. Furthermore, the few people who manage to discover this reality almost never learn that there is something unlimited—the Self—for which to strive. As such, we continue to try to squeeze as much happiness as we can out of whatever limited objects we can attain. Only when, through grace, we hear of the potential for transcendence through realizing the Self, does our inherent mumukṣutvam gain the power to help us. Moreover, it is only at this point that the strength of our mumukṣutvam, or lack thereof, is revealed to us. Only if it has some substance will we begin trying to cultivate viveka [discrimination] and vairāgya [dispassion]. Otherwise, we will continue to pursue happiness through the limited material world.

In general, these three qualities are strengthened through the performance of *karma yoga*. Karma yoga is not a particular action, but an attitude that can be applied to any action. In essence the attitude is one of total care with regards to action and one of total acceptance with regards to the results of those actions. (Karma yoga will be discussed in detail in Chapter Five.) This attitude is easier said than done, especially when our main motivations for performing actions are material results—i.e. money, name and fame, etc. Therefore, it is much easier to implement the karma-yoga attitude when our engagement in the work is not born out of our own desire, but simply because our guru has told us to do that job. This is one of the reasons why, after some time, Amma usually suggests that we do some form of work. It could be cleaning the kitchen, tending the cows, cleaning public places or parks, helping with our local Amma Satsaṅg group's newsletter or even working for Amma's university or hospital. Sometimes it is even serving Amma directly. Through such work, we begin to get a feel for performing work as karma yoga. It may be a 60-hour-per-week job or just an hour or two on weekends. Whatever it may be, we gradually develop the ability to use the karma-yoga attitude in all aspects of life—whether it is at a salaried position for a multinational corporation or family chores.

Guru seva—selfless service instructed by the guru—is not a form of slavery. Nor is it something we do in exchange for Amma's teachings and affection. The guru is one with the divine truth that pervades creation. As such, Amma doesn't need us to wash pots or help chop vegetables at her programs. Nor does she need us to help with any of the Āśram's selfless-service projects. In fact Amma doesn't need us to serve anyone at all. She is complete with or without such things. Amma offers us the opportunities to do such things because of the infinite good she knows such actions, if done with love and care and sincerity, will bring us. She knows their power to purify our mind of its likes and dislikes—to cultivate dispassion for the transient pleasures of the senses and to bring passion for the eternal bliss of the Self—all of which are essential if we are to attain true freedom.

In fact, there is another unique way in which Amma helps everyone cultivate mumukṣutvam and vairāgya, and that is her *darśan.* In the tenderness of Amma's embrace, our mind is suddenly silenced, allowing the peace and bliss of our True Self to shine forth. For many that experience is a real eye-opener—a deliverance. As said previously, it transforms our thinking and reshuffles our goals. Amma's darśan helps us to experience a profound peace unassociated with any sense object—a peace coming from within. For the spiritual seeker, the memory of this experience becomes like the proverbial carrot, directing them ever forward. As one sannyāsi who visited the āśram once commented, "Darśan is an experience after which one wishes to experience nothing but that ever again."

A devotee once explained the effect of Amma's darśan in the following way. When she was young her parents did not want her to eat chocolate. Instead they would give her carob and tell her it was chocolate. For years she went on eating carob and thinking it was chocolate. And then inevitably someone gave her real chocolate. Thereafter she was never satisfied with carob ever again. It is the same with Amma's darśan. Amma says that when people have her darśan it is like drinking crystal-clear spring water after a lifetime of attempting to quench their thirst with sewage water. So, to some extent, Amma is helping us refine our minds and perspectives right from the beginning.

The remaining areas of required mental refinement are together referred to as śamādi ṣatka sampatti—the six-fold disciplines beginning with mental control[5]. These are *śama, dama, uparama, titikṣa, śraddha* and *samādhāna.*

DAMA

We will start with dama—developing control over our senses. In the beginning stages of spiritual life, our mind is weak and can

[5] During *ārati,* Amma's skill at helping her children develop these qualities is extolled through the name *śama-dama dāyini*—she who gives mind control and sense control.

be easily disturbed by many sense objects. We are trying to live up to the truth that we ourselves are the source of all bliss. However after so many lifetimes of exclusively seeking and, however fleetingly, experiencing bliss through the objects of the world, this is not so easy. Thus, dama literally means avoiding contact with sense objects that will disturb our mind. In the Bhagavad-Gīta, the example of the turtle is given:

> yadā saṁharate cāyaṁ kūrmo'ṅgānīva sarvaśaḥ |
> indriyāṇīndriyārthebhyaḥ tasya prajña pratiṣṭhitā ||

> *"When, as a turtle withdraws its limbs, he withdraws his senses from the sense objects, his wisdom is then set firm."* [Bhagavad-Gīta, 2.58]

Whenever danger comes, the turtle immediately pulls in its head and four legs. Shut off from the outside world, it is safe until the source of potential harm passes. In the same way, the spiritual seeker must avoid allowing his five sense organs—eyes, ears, nose, touch and taste—to come into contact with potentially harmful sense objects.

For example, if we are on a diet and there are two ways home from work—one of which passes by the Pizza Hut and Ben & Jerry's Ice Cream parlor—picking the other way is dama. Or, as spiritual aspirants, if we are riding on a bus and the people in front of us are engaged in worldly conversation, we can slip on our headphones and listen to some *bhajans* or to some spiritual talks. In the worst-case scenario, if there is something we know it is better that we do not see, we can simply close our eyes. All these are forms of sense control.

Along these lines I've heard a nice joke about a man demonstrating dama. A customer in a bakery was carefully examining all the rich-looking pastries displayed on trays in the glass cases. When the clerk approached him and asked, "What would you like?" he answered, "I'd like that chocolate-covered, cream-filled doughnut, that jelly-filled doughnut and that cheese Danish." Then with a sigh he added, "But I'll take an oat-bran muffin."

In Amṛtapuri, the āśramites have to follow many rules. These rules are all aimed at helping them gain control over their senses. What does not enter the senses, cannot easily enter the mind. Amma has made these rules with their higher good in mind. They have come to the āśram with a particular goal, and Amma wants to help them attain it.

Psychologists often criticize monastic restrictions, claiming they are a form of repression and that repression can cause health problems and insanity. They are partly right. *Repression* can result in such maladies. However, the spiritual seeker's dama is not one of repression. Rather it is *sublimation*. It is based on his knowledge that the impulse to indulge the senses is an obstacle to his higher goal. In this regard, Amma says it is like a student forgoing hanging out with his friends in order to study for an exam, or like a diabetic avoiding sugar. His avoidance is born out of his understanding, his discriminative thinking. Therefore his mind and his body are in harmony, and there is never any breakdown. If a child believes his teddy bear protects him from monsters that live in the closet and we force him to throw it away, there can easily be a negative impact upon his psyche. However, when the child outgrows this delusion and decides on his own to stop sleeping with the stuffed animal, obviously there is no harm in it. Proper dama is based upon understanding—the knowledge that sense objects are inherently worthless—not upon the idea that they are 'evil' in a moralistic sense.

One day a certain monk, who'd been locked in a cell performing austerities for decades, became very sick. Many doctors came to see him but no one could diagnose his illness. Finally a psychiatrist came. After a short discussion, the psychiatrist told him his problem was suppression. "For 20 years you have forsaken the world, rejecting all worldly pleasures," the psychologist said.

"You need to loosen up and live a little. I suggest you get out of your cell and take a nice drive through the country."

"It's not possible!" said the monk. "I have renounced all such things. I have taken vows! Mine is a life of *austerity*—not joyrides!"

The psychiatrist remained firm, telling the monk it was either loosen up or die. The monk closed his eyes in contemplation. Ten seconds later he opened his eyes. "Okay," he sighed. "But get me a Benz convertible with plush leather seats and a killer stereo."

Our sense control has to be based on understanding. If we merely repress our desires, they will only build up and eventually overpower us.

ŚAMA

The next discipline is śama—control over the mind. Of course it is impossible to close ourselves off entirely from potentially dangerous sense objects. Whether we like it or not, some will enter our mind through the senses and make an impression. Once the impression has entered, it will continue to come back into the conscious mind from time to time. And even if we somehow avoid seeing and hearing the spiritually inauspicious, our minds are fully capable of negativity on their own accord. We have all had the experience of falling victim to negative thoughts. Say we suddenly find ourself thinking negatively about an acquaintance, co-worker or family member—perhaps being overly critical of some personality flaw of his. This is where śama comes in. Although these impulse thoughts cannot be prevented, they can be nipped in the bud. One method of śama is simply replacing the negative thought with a positive thought. This can be the chanting of our *mantra*, a memory of an interaction we've had with Amma, or consciously thinking of a good quality possessed by that person.

Another method Amma recommends is intellectually knocking the negative thought out of our heads by asking ourselves,

"Will this thought really help me in life? Will it help society? Is thinking about this going to help me reach my goal in life? If I only see other people's negativities, how will I ever experience a sense of unity with all creation?" Thinking in this way, we can also destroy the potentially harmful thought.

Now the question is, how can Amma's guru bhāva help us here? In regards to dama, it seems possible. Amma can impose restrictions. But inside the privacy of our own heads, can Amma intervene? The answer is yes. When it comes to the seva done by the āśramites, Amma can be quite a taskmaster. If she becomes aware of work that is done carelessly, she definitely will summon the concerned party. The scolding that ensues will make an impression on the person's mind, which will make them more aware when performing their actions in the future. Or rather than scold someone, Amma will punish herself—usually by fasting. If we have even a little love for Amma, such heartbreaking incidents make a much deeper impact than any scolding ever could.

Back when I was working for the bank, I sometimes used to smoke. Actually one of the main reasons I did it was to help remain alert during work after staying up all night during Amma's Devi and Kṛṣṇa Bhāva darśans. Nevertheless, it was beginning to become a habit. Then one night—during the short break between the two bhāva darśans—I went to get Amma a cup of tea from a nearby devotee's house-cum-tea-stall. Standing outside, I thought I could have a quick smoke while I waited for the milk to boil. So I did so. When the tea was ready, I put out my cigarette, washed my hands, rinsed my mouth, and took the cup to Amma. As soon as I handed it to her, she said, "You smoked a cigarette, didn't you?" I admitted I had. Amma looked at me with an expression of uneasiness and said, "Then I don't want it." I felt really bad because that single cup of tea was the only form of sustenance Amma would typically take all night long. Now, because of my actions, she wasn't even going to drink that.

The next day at work I began craving a cigarette. But when I did so, I immediately thought of Amma looking at me with that expression and saying, "I don't want it." I also thought of how she had fasted all night long. I decided not to smoke. This wasn't a one-time occurrence. Thereafter, every time I considered smoking, I thought of Amma's fast. Soon I had given up smoking altogether.

So when Amma invokes her guru bhāva and scolds us or punishes herself, it makes a deep impression in our mind. The desire to avoid another such encounter with Amma in the future creates extra awareness in us and extreme attention to detail with regards to that action. Thus our work becomes like a meditation. Although cultivated through heightened attention to *external* detail, this awareness will be available with regard to *internal* details as well. And this internal awareness is essential for successful śama. For only if we are immediately aware of the presence of a harmful thought or impulse can we remove it through chanting our mantra or exercising our discriminative thinking. So Amma the disciplinarian can help us in this regard as well.

UPARAMA

Uparama is steadfast performance of one's *dharma* [duty], whatever that may be. The dharma of a householder is obviously different than that of a brahmacāri or sannyāsi. But as Amma's children, there are dharmas that are common to all of us, including the daily performance of *arcana*, the chanting of our mantra a certain number of times, meditation, seva, etc. In fact for us, Amma's children, everything Amma tells us to do is our dharma. In the āśram, Amma has her special ways of helping the brahmacāris to maintain regularity in such practices. Here is one example: Recently Amma came to know that a number of brahmacāris had been missing the morning arcana—the chanting of the Lalita

Sahasranāma[6], etc., that begins at 4:50 every morning. That Tuesday, when all the āśram residents came for Amma's *prasād*, Amma read out the names of all of those who'd been absent. All the guilty parties were then made to come forward. "This is an āśram," Amma said. "The rules and regulations here are for your benefit. Now you will have to pay the penalty. You must now take your plate and, banging it with your spoon, walk around the āśram grounds singing, 'I will attend arcana; I will not repeat this mistake! I will attend arcana; I will not repeat this mistake!' Soon the āśram was filled with the sounds of steel spoons banging on steel plates and the timid singing of 10 or so brahmacāris. After they returned, Amma said, "We are all nursery-school students in spirituality. We need to follow some rules and regulations. We all have pride in our body and appearance. We will remember this punishment and that will give us some awareness next time. Through the cultivation of awareness, we can become so alert that even the smallest negative thought will not be able to enter our mind without our knowledge of it. This is the level of awareness that is needed."

TITIKṢA

Titikṣa is the ability to maintain patience and even-mindedness when undergoing the various experiences of life, such as heat and cold, pleasure and pain, etc. In short, this means learning to adjust one's mind to the current situation. One of the best examples of Amma instilling titikṣa takes place on her India tours. During these tours, the āśramites ride on buses. Inevitably, the seats will leave something to be desired in terms of leg-room, seat padding and shock-absorption. Sometimes āśramites even take turns standing due to lack of seats. The aisles of the buses are often stacked with an assortment of pots, pans, boxes, trunks and loudspeakers. In some places the roads are quite nice, but in others it feels like

[6] The Thousand Names of the Divine Mother

riding up and down the craters of the moon! And temperatures during the day get very hot, and there is no AC. What is this all about? In fact it is one of Amma's ways of helping her disciples increase their tolerance levels. Pain is relative. What one person considers excruciatingly painful, a person with a strong mind merely shrugs off. If left to their own devices, no one would take such a journey. However, we see that due to the golden opportunities to spend time with Amma, not only do the āśram residents look forward to these tours, but devotees come from all over the world in order to participate. Understanding the need for such austerities, they willingly undergo them and conclude the tour much tougher mentally.

ŚRADDHA

Śraddha is trust and faith in the words of the guru and the scriptures. We may feel like we have a lot of faith, but upon close inspection we often see that our faith is quite limited. Amma says, "These days, our faith is like an artificial limb. It has no vitality. We have no heartfelt connection with faith, for it has not been ingrained properly in our lives."

Once a man was walking in the mountains, enjoying the scenery, when he stepped too close to the edge of a cliff and started to fall. In desperation he reached out and grabbed a limb of an old tree growing out of the side of the cliff. Full of fear, he assessed his situation. He was about 100 feet down a sheer cliff and about 900 feet from the floor of the canyon below. He cried out, "Help me!" But there was no answer. Again and again he cried out, all to no avail. Finally he yelled, "Is anybody up there?"

Suddenly a deep voice replied, "Yes, I'm up here."

"Who is it?"

"It's God."

"Can you help me?"

"Yes, I can help. Have faith in me."

"Okay, I have faith. Now, help me—*please*!"

The deep voice responded, "Okay. I want you to have faith in me and let go."

Looking around the man became full of panic. He couldn't believe his ears. "What?"

The voice repeated itself, "Have faith in me. Let go. I will catch you."

At this point the man called out, "Uh... Is there anyone else up there?"

Faith is not something that can be forced through discipline. However, Amma does help foster such faith within us. For when a realized master speaks, the words have a power of authority like no one else's. This is because the truths they proclaim are 100 percent their own experience. No scripture, philosopher or scholar will make such an impact. The sadguru's every action and word reflect the fact that he is established in the ultimate truth and that it is possible for each of us to realize that Truth for ourselves.

Moreover, in spiritual life we find that trust cultivates more trust. In Indian culture, faith is cultivated from the child's very entrance into the world. *Samskāras*—birth rites, naming ceremonies, first-feeding rituals, educational ceremonies, wedding rites, etc.—are woven throughout life in such a manner that one steadily becomes more and more grounded in the power and validity of the religious and spiritual tradition. By the time one comes to the guru, deep faith in spiritual principles has already been ingrained within one through one's own experience. Under the guidance of the guru, this faith continues to mature. For example, often the guru will ask us to undertake a task that is outside our comfort zone. Perhaps, he will ask us to perform a job for which we feel totally unqualified. If we have trust in the guru and act without hesitation, we will discover our fears were unfounded. This will boost our faith even further. On the other hand, if we succumb to our inhibitions and refrain from following the guru's words, our fears only grow stronger. When guided by faith, the mind is an excellent servant. But when we allow it to call the shots, it becomes a tyrannical master.

SAMĀDHĀNA

Samādhāna is perfection in one-pointed concentration. This is only possible through the performance of spiritual practices given by the guru, such as meditation, *mantra japa* and other forms of chanting and singing. (These will be discussed in detail in Chapter Eight.) Until our yearning for liberation is fully ignited, if left to our own devices, our regularity in such practices may somewhat waver. However in the āśram Amma makes a strict schedule for all the disciples to follow, helping them gain perfection in one-pointed focus.

Concentration is not only needed in terms of being able to focus in meditation or on the words of our guru. It is also needed in terms of attaining the goal of one's life. This type of concentration Amma refers to as *lakṣya bodha*—awareness of the goal. In Amma's āśram you will find many places—in the elevators, on computer monitors, on steering wheels—where people have put small stickers saying, "Remember to chant your mantra." Every thought we have of the guru can serve as such a sticker if we have the right attitude.

WE SHOULD NOT THINK that one day Amma will call us forward and announce to us that today marks the beginning of our guru-disciple relationship. It is not like that. Assessing the maturity, surrender, dispassion and thirst for the goal in each person, Amma acts accordingly, always taking the big picture into account. Some are ready more or less immediately; others need a little more time in the oven, so to speak. There are no black-and-whites. To what extent we are ready for disciplining, Amma will give. Besides, everyone is different—not everyone requires Amma's direct discipline. There are people who have been in the āśram for 20 years whom Amma has never directly corrected in any way. At the same time there are devotees who have never set foot in Amṛtapuri with whom Amma is very strict almost right from the start. It all goes to show that Amma is looking at a bigger picture than we have eyes to see, taking into consideration each person's past, present and future, and acting accordingly.

Amma says that we cannot set a general list of rules for how the guru will treat a disciple. "The guru leads the disciple according to the *vāsanas* [tendencies] the disciple has acquired during many lifetimes," Amma says. "Even in identical situations, the guru may behave quite differently toward different disciples. It won't necessarily make any sense to you. Only the guru will know the reason. The guru decides which procedures to follow in order to weaken the vāsanas of a particular individual and to lead him or her to the goal. The one factor that will help the disciple's spiritual progress is that he or she yield to the guru's decisions. When two disciples make the same mistake, the master may get angry with one of them and be very loving toward the other, acting as though nothing has happened."

Ultimately the guru is chipping away at the disciple's ego. It is like a master sculptor chipping away at a massive piece of rock. From the perspective of the rock, it may seem very painful, but the master can see the beautiful image of God waiting inside. It is not a process that can be rushed. The guru proceeds cautiously. It is a process that can only be done by a master craftsman. Others will only crack the stone and mar the beauty of the image waiting inside.

The only difference between a stone and a disciple is that the stone has no choice but to surrender. The disciple can always get fed up and leave, which sometimes happens. Some of the places the guru hits can be very painful. And a sadguru like Amma knows all the right spots! In India there are people called *mārmikas*—people who know all the body's minute pressure points and can disable a person with the mere tap of a finger. In many ways, Amma is like this. In one sentence she can render us powerless. Furthermore she has the power to obscure this from everyone else around. To everyone else it will seem like a big joke, another one of Amma's *līlas* [divine plays], or even a *compliment.* Only Amma's target will know how sharp and precise her arrow had been.

I remember an incident that happened several years ago. Amma was giving darśan and one devotee asked, "Amma, whenever I come to the āśram I hear so many beautiful bhajans. Where are all these bhajans coming from? Who is writing them?"

Amma responded, "So many people are writing the bhajans—devotees, brahmacāris, brahmacārinis, swāmis..." Then, gesturing over at one brahmacāri sitting near her, Amma said, "He has written some very beautiful songs."

Ostensibly, Amma was paying this brahmacāri a compliment. But in truth it was a precise blow landed by Amma's chisel. Indeed, the brahmacāri had written several bhajans and given them to Amma, but Amma had yet to sing any of them. In fact, a week before he had confronted Amma regarding this issue, saying, "Amma, I've offered you so many bhajans, but you've never sung any of them! Other people give you bhajans, which I know are not as good as mine, and you immediately start singing them. I know it is just because you love them more than you love me."

Amma had responded, "Son, you say that you 'offered' these songs to Amma, but did you really? If one truly offers something to someone, then it is no longer theirs. It now belongs to the one to whom it has been offered. This is true offering. Your 'offering' seems to have many conditions attached to it."

Aesthetically and technically, the bhajans composed by this brahmacāri may have been of a superior quality. However, as his guru, Amma's primary concern was not singing excellent bhajans but teaching him a lesson regarding ego[7], which manifests as the

[7] A few weeks later Amma did indeed begin singing some of the brahmacāri's bhajans.

feeling of doership. Amma always has our highest good in mind. In fact, even though they can be painful, such experiences are precious. Amma is taking the time to chisel, to correct, to polish.

I remember once reading a verse in praise of the guru which read:

If you feel like a mouse
whose tail has been trapped under the paw of a cat,
know that the guru is holding you
most dearly in his heart.

We should always keep this understanding alive within us. Otherwise, like the brahmacāri who 'offered' Amma the songs, we may begin to judge the guru, erroneously believing her actions to be arising from a set of likes and dislikes and not our highest good.

I remember a family who used to live in the āśram. Externally they were close with Amma. But when Amma's guru bhāva arose with them, they quickly packed up and left, telling people, "Guruvāyūrappan[8] is enough for us!" Devotees of God always pray for God to take form and visit them. But when he does, before long they often wish he would go back to where he came from!

THE INNER GURU

Not only does a sadguru point out our defects, but he also helps us to see them on our own. Gradually the world begins becoming more and more like a mirror in which all of our negativities and character flaws are reflected. In fact, Amma says the external guru's goal is to help us awaken the inner guru. When we develop this level of tuning, the whole world becomes the guru. We see the teachings we've learned from the external guru everywhere we look—in our family life, professional life, social life, even in Nature. This is how Amma says it was for her, even as a child.

[8] Śrī Kṛṣṇa as installed in a famous Kerala temple near Triśśūr.

"Everything in this world is Amma's guru," Amma says. "God and the guru are within every person. But as long as the ego persists, we remain unaware of this. The ego acts like a veil and hides the inner guru. Once you discover the inner guru, you will perceive the guru in everything in the universe. As Amma found the guru within herself, everything, including each grain of sand, became her guru. You may wonder then if even a thorn was Amma's guru. Yes, every thorn was her guru; for when your foot is pricked by a thorn, you pay greater attention to the path. Thus, that thorn helps you to avoid being pricked by other thorns and to avoid falling into a deep ditch. Amma also looks upon her body as a guru; because when we contemplate the impermanent nature of the body we come to realize that the Self is the only eternal reality. Everything around Amma led her to goodness, and because of this, Amma feels a sense of reverence toward everything in life."

It is the job of the external guru to take us to this point. But it is not that the guru abandons us once we reach there. On the contrary, the guru is then with us constantly—eating with us, walking with us, working with us, even sleeping with us. This is because the guru's teachings have become one with us and, everywhere our mind goes, they come along. Furthermore, the knowledge that the guru's essence—consciousness—is pervading the cosmos is also with us. Once we reach this point, it is as if we are on the express train. There is no getting off—one's whole life is lived in communion with the sadguru.

Chapter Four:

The Role of Amma's Āśram

"An āśram is not a mere cluster of inanimate buildings, temples and trees; rather it is the very embodiment of the sadguru's grace. It is a vital, dynamic and living institution that stimulates the aspiration of the sincere student to attain the state of oneness."

—Amma

FOR SOMEONE INTERESTED in spiritual progress, no place is more conducive than the *āśram* of an enlightened master. Amṛtapuri is like a university—the perfect place to learn, practice and assimilate the spiritual teachings. Once one reaches here, there is no need to go anywhere else.

Even though Amṛtapuri often seems more festival ground than hermitage, Amma is providing everything we need for our spiritual growth—on both the physical and subtle levels. In this regard, Amma's āśram is intentionally a microcosm of the 'real world,' where we will come across all types of people and situations. If we have the right attitude, this will help us mature spiritually. The āśram experience can be compared to learning to swim in a pool versus diving directly into the ocean. Remaining under the protective eye of master lifeguard Amma, we can learn and gradually perfect all the strokes needed to stay afloat in life. Thereafter, we can swim anywhere. As Amma says, "For one who has mastered swimming, the waves of the ocean present only a delightful game, but for one who doesn't know how to swim, they are terrifying and may result in his death."

For many the first time they visit Amma's āśram is like a homecoming. They've never been there before, yet they feel like, for the first time in their lives, they have truly come home. At the time of this book's publication[1], there are more than 3,000 full-time āśram residents—a mix of *sannyāsis*, *brahmacāris* and *brahmacārinis* and householders—living in Amṛtapuri. On top of that, Amṛtapuri, being one of the five campuses of Amṛta University, is also home to approximately 3,000 college students. Furthermore, on any given day, hundreds of devotees are visiting from around the world. Some stay for as long as six months. Then there are the thousands of people who come just for the day in order to have Amma's *darśan*. In many ways an āśram that was once simply the home of Amma's parents has been transformed into a full-fledged village.

Amma often compares the āśram to a large joint family. In India the tradition is such that when a son marries, his wife comes to live with him and his parents—if not in the same house, in the same compound. Some such compounds are enormous. I remember in 2007 Amma visited a place like this next to the Śrī Raṅganāthan Temple in Tiruccirapaḷḷi, Tamil Nādu. There must have been 70 relatives living together in one housing complex. But really that is nothing. In Lakkūr, Karṇāṭaka, there's one family with 170 members living together! In the old days, most Indian families were like this. Now, the nuclear family has come into favor. The prevailing attitude is that two parents and their children are more than enough to have under one roof. And as soon as the children are old enough, they want to move out and get their own place. But Amma says that if we look, we see that children raised in joint families generally become more mature and mentally resilient than the 'only child' or even children raised with just one or two siblings.

[1] 2009

Living in Amṛtapuri is like this, yet to the nth degree. In the joint-family system everyone speaks the same language and has the same culture. In Amṛtapuri, you have people from more than 50 different countries, speaking dozens of languages! Amma compares so many different types of people living and working together to throwing hundreds of rough stones into a giant rock-tumbler. As the stones bump and bash and crash against one another, all their rough edges are worn away. In the end the stones come out smooth, polished and shining.

In the world today, we see just the opposite. Everyone is hiding from one another. The employee is hiding from the boss. The husband is hiding from the wife. The wife is hiding from the husband. The children are hiding from the parents, and the parents are hiding from the children! As Amma says, "If there are four people in a house, they all live like isolated islands."

This reminds me of a cartoon a devotee once showed me. In the drawing was the wife—a big, heavyset woman carrying a rolling pin. She was peering under a bed and shouting, "If you're a man, come out from under there!" And who was under the bed? The husband. He was small and skinny, and was squeezing himself into the very corner under the far side of the bed. From there, he was shouting back, "I'm the man of the house! I'll come out whenever I want!"

We think our isolation is one of choice, but really we are just allowing our insecurity and over-sensitivity to box us in. We claim 'the space under the bed' with a great sense of victory, blissfully unaware that we are cutting ourselves off from the rest of the house!

Today everyone wants their own room, their own office and their own car. In our hands, even devices invented to enhance connectivity—like mobile phones and the Internet—are only serving to allow us to insulate and isolate ourselves more than ever before. The result is a generation utterly unable to face the smallest of difficulties with mental equanimity. When conflict does occur, we either sink into depression or fly into a rage. In our isolated world, there is no one to keep our ego and selfishness in check. We become completely self-oriented, unable to consider the feelings and views of others.

In 2007 Amma delivered an address at the Cinema Verite Film Festival in Paris titled *Compassion: The Only Way to Peace*. In that speech, Amma spoke at length about the disharmony between humanity and Nature. She also gave a list of many actions people can implement to begin rectifying the situation. One of these suggestions was to carpool. After listing all the immediate benefits—less pollution, less oil consumption, less traffic, etc.—Amma said, "Most importantly, love and cooperation will increase amongst people." So, clearly Amma sees this self-isolation as having a serious negative impact on the minds of individuals and on society as a whole. Life in the āśram works on the same principle; it's like one big carpool.

The āśram provides an ideal environment to perform our spiritual practices. As we will see in later chapters, we can basically divide spiritual practices into three: *karma yoga*, meditation and the pursuit of Self-knowledge. As we will discuss in more detail in Chapter Five, karma yoga is aimed primarily at helping us attain *vairāgya*—overcoming our likes and dislikes so that we can have at least a relative level of mental equanimity. For this spiritual practice, there is no better place than Amṛtapuri. In order to overcome something, we first must be made aware of its presence. In Amṛtapuri, there is nowhere to cloister ourselves—no beds to hide under. If one insists on holding on to his likes and dislikes, Amṛtapuri may very well not be a comfortable place. On the other hand if one understands that likes and dislikes are limitations and ultimately undesirable, Amṛtapuri becomes the perfect training ground.

In the āśram the opportunity for *tapas* [self-accepted austerity] is also all-pervading. You can learn patience standing in the line for food or to have Amma's darśan. You can practice *titikṣa* [indifference to difficulty] wading upstream through the crowds of people on festival days like Oṇam and Amma's birthday. You can overcome your dependence upon sleep, staying up to be with Amma. You can overcome your dependence upon tasty food. You can discover you don't really need a plush bed in your own room to sleep upon, but can sleep like a baby on a straw mat with a couple of other people in a 12x12-foot room. You can overcome your aversion to noise and learn to be peaceful in all environments.

Someone once told me the following joke about a country wherein everything took a long time to accomplish. A man needs a car, so he goes to a car-dealer who shows him two models. He chooses the one he wants and pays for the car. The car-dealer says, "Your car will be ready for you to pick it up exactly 10 years from today."

The man responds, "Oh, in the morning or the afternoon?"

The car-dealer says, "What does it matter?"

The man replies, "Well, the plumber is coming in the morning."

The point is not that the āśram is like an inefficiently run country. Nor is it that we should suffer unnecessarily. Rather the idea is that positive qualities such as patience can be developed if we take challenging situations in stride and face them with a positive attitude. On top of this, Amma's presence and vibration help our mind stay focused despite the challenges that arise.

With regard to the second spiritual practice, meditation, Amritapuri is also a blessed place. It's almost a paradox. How can a place, buzzing like a beehive with noise and activity, be conducive for meditation? When people first visit Amṛtapuri, this is a common doubt. However, if they hold on for a few days, they soon find themselves gaining an internal peace, despite the external commotion. Even though there may be 10,000 people in the āśram, it still has a feeling of solitude. This is something that can only be attributed to the presence of Amma—a living master. In fact, it is also Amma's presence that helps us to let go of our likes and dislikes, and surrender through karma yoga. The presence of a fully enlightened soul is something utterly unique and transformative.

"However much we may dig in certain places, we will not necessarily find water," Amma says. "On the other hand, if we dig beside a river we can easily get water; we won't have to dig very deep. Similarly, the proximity of a sadguru makes the spiritual task easier for you as a disciple. You will be able to enjoy the fruits of your practices without much effort."

Having realized the ultimate truth, Amma's mind is ever saturated with bliss. Her mind is so pure, it radiates a vibration of peace and tranquility. This vibration spans outward and affects the minds of those in Amma's proximity. It pervades the entire āśram. This is why many people immediately feel more relaxed and peaceful upon entering the āśram grounds. Even journalists with no spiritual inclination whatsoever often comment on this experience. It is like the phenomenon of sympathetic vibration, wherein an entity vibrating at a certain frequency causes other separate entities to begin vibrating at that same frequency as well. It is nothing but this phenomenon that is symbolized in paintings of various saints, wherein lions and lambs are portrayed as lying peaceful, side by side. The fear of the lamb and the ferocity of the lion are neutralized by the powerful, peaceful vibration of the *mahātma's* mind.

All types of people come to the āśram. Some just hop off the tourist boat as it comes down the backwaters. Often such people visibly carry the weight of the world upon their shoulders. Even though they are on vacation, you can tell that the burdens of life are weighing very heavily upon many of them. When I see such people, I have to admit, my interest is piqued. Why? Because I know if they stay for a week or two, we will see such a transformation in them. They will begin to walk differently, talk differently, smile differently... They will seem healthier, physically and mentally. A special light comes to their face, where before there were mainly dark clouds. I can only attribute this to the deep and powerful vibration radiating from Amma. And it is this powerful vibration that makes our mind naturally meditative. This is why around Amma people find it much easier to chant their mantras with focus, visualize their chosen objects of meditation and remain focused on God in general.

With regards to *jñāna yoga*, again Amṛtapuri provides an ideal environment. Not only is Amma regularly giving talks and conducting question-and-answer sessions, but there are also regular classes on core scriptures like the upaniṣads, Bhagavad-Gīta and Brahma Sūtras. The rare beauty of Amma's question-and-answer sessions is that Amma does not restrict anyone from asking any question. Furthermore, she always answers according to the questioner's level of understanding. Such tailor-made responses are simply unavailable in books. Amṛtapuri is the perfect place to study the scriptures, clear one's doubts and ultimately assimilate spiritual knowledge. In the peace of Amma's āśram, one is more readily reflective, more readily able to function from various degrees of *sākṣi bhāva* [the mood of a witness] and to contemplate the truth of the Self.

Amma says that the soil of Amṛtapuri has been tilled with her very teardrops—the austerities she performed and continues to perform for the benefit of the world. This is what has rendered the earth here sacred. As such, Amṛtapuri is the most fertile ground one can find for the cultivation of *bhakti*—devotion to God. Amma does not define bhakti as devotion to a specific form of God. Rather she says it is the purest form of love—a love without boundaries, expectations or restrictions. Its culmination is in totally surrendering ourselves to the divine. Depending on the stage of the seeker's development, devotion will manifest in different ways, but the inner feeling ever remains; it only grows stronger. Many come to Amṛtapuri not even understanding the meaning of the word 'devotion,' but bhakti soon takes birth within them nonetheless. Listening to Amma's heartfelt *bhajans*, seeing her rapture in calling out the names of God, we soon find ourselves transformed, our hearts expanding in love for God. Bhakti transforms from an abstract concept to the center of who we are.

Just walking around in the āśram we feel inspired to engage in and persevere with our spiritual practices. In almost every way, it is the exact opposite of our family homes. The family, at most, has one small room dedicated to God, the rest to family. The āśram is like living inside an enormous *pūja* room[2]. A family home is set up for our comfort. The pictures of family members on the walls, the mementos of our holidays, the television, the soft sofa... everything is a constant reminder of our limited persona and a call to embrace comfort through the senses. In our homes, often we are the only one who wants to wake up early, chant *arcana*, practice meditation, study the scriptures, etc. When we are in silence, the family has a party. When we are trying to fast, they cook our favorite dish. I remember someone once showed me a cartoon along these lines. Sitting in his middleclass bedroom was a teenager dressed as a *brahmacāri*—robes, head shaved except for the tuft, a tambourine for bhajans in his hand. Standing in the doorway were his parents, who didn't look very pleased about their son's chosen direction in life. The caption read: "Your father and I just want you to know that we're behind you 100 percent should you decide to go back to being a drug addict."

The āśram is just the opposite. In the āśram all the pictures are of gods or mahātmas. Everywhere you look, you see people dressed in the uniforms of purity and renunciation. Everything is soaked with the memory of Amma. Her footprints cover the āśram grounds. We see the backwaters and are reminded of the time we saw Amma cross it on the village boat, or the stories we've heard Amma tell about swimming with her childhood friends. We see the ocean and think of Amma sitting on the water's edge blissfully singing "Sṛṣṭiyum Nīye." And of course, whenever

[2] In India, one room of the house is traditionally dedicated for prayer, meditation and worship.

she is at the āśram, one can go anytime and watch Amma as she gives darśan. Bhajans with Amma every night! There is no more inspiring atmosphere than the āśram of a living master.

Here, there is the power of *saṅgha*—spiritual company. Everyone is waking early. Everyone is meditating. Everyone is attending the bhajans, etc. People help each other wake for the chanting when they sleep through the morning bell, etc. This helps us to persevere at times when, if left to our own devices, we would give up. It is like learning the alphabet in a school as opposed to all alone.

FOUR STAGES OF LIFE

The Vedic plan for life involves four *āśramas* [stages of life]: *brahmacārya āśrama, gṛhasta āśrama, vānaprastha āśrama* and *sannyāsa āśrama*[3]. According to this system, boys (from approximately age seven to 20) went to live in an āśram, living as a brahmacāri and receiving education—both secular and non-secular—from the guru. Thereafter, the majority went on to gṛhasta āśrama [householder life], while the rare few who had the dispassion to avoid marriage, went directly into sannyāsa āśrama [monastic life]. Householder life was not entered to become mired in one's desires. It was used as a vehicle to fulfill desires to some extent, but also to purify one's mind through karma yoga. Thereby, one developed the maturity that comes with understanding that permanent happiness can never come through fulfilling one's desires. After the couple's children were raised and they were free of responsibilities, they left their home to pursue a life of meditation in the forest—vānaprastha āśrama. Finally, when mentally prepared, they even cut their bond as husband and wife and sannyāsa āśrama was entered.

---

[3] The four *āśramas* [stages of life] are student life, householder life, hermit life and monkhood, respectively.

For various reasons, this system has all but completely deteriorated during the past couple of centuries. Amma says that trying to revive it would only result in failure. Rather than trying to recreate the past, we should focus on how to move forward while preserving our traditional values as much as possible. It is with this aim that Amma's āśram has come—creating a space wherein people from all walks of life can live and pursue the various spiritual practices originally carried out in the four āśramas.

Āśram life is not for running away from our responsibilities. Once we have committed to a path in life, we should see it to its proper end. In Amma's āśram, the main people who join as brahmacāris or brahmacārinis are college graduates who have yet to marry. Being in their twenties, these people join with the intention of dedicating their entire life to the spiritual path. They do not take external vows, but it is their intention. They are joining the āśram as opposed to entering married life. Amma often recommends that those interested in such a life first spend a year or so living in the āśram, seeing how their mind responds to its rules and regulations. Afterward, if they feel they have the requisite dispassion, they can join. After living in the āśram for many years, some of these are formally initiated into brahmacārya and are given yellow robes by Amma herself. The brahmacāris and brahmacārinis are monks in training. They live according to strict rules of conduct, study the scriptures and purify their minds through *seva* and meditation.

Other than the brahmacāris and brahmacārinis, Amṛtapuri is also home to hundreds of families—both from India and abroad—who have decided to live and raise their children here. Some of them maintain jobs outside. Others are in a position to dedicate themselves fully to the āśram's various seva projects and institutions. There are also many retired couples living in the āśram as well. So the gṛhastāśrami [householder] and vānaprastha āśrami [retired hermit] also have a home in Amṛtapuri.

Finally, there are the sannyāsis, former brahmacāris who have been initiated under Amma's instruction directly into a life of total renunciation, no longer living for selfish motives but completely dedicating themselves to serving the world. Amma's opinion is that a sannyāsi should make a vow to serve the world selflessly. He is supposed to understand that he is not the body, mind or intellect, and therefore he should establish himself in the *ātma* [Self]. Speaking at a congregation of sannyāsis in 2007[4], Amma presented her vision of *sannyāsa*. She said, "A real sannyāsi is one who can remain content even while performing any action. *Ātma samarpaṇam* [Self-surrender] is the secret to happiness. This means that a sannyāsi should be able to perform actions without attachment. Such non-attachment is only possible through surrender. A compassion-filled heart, the readiness to sacrifice one's self spawned by such a heart, and the happiness that ensues from thus sacrificing one's comforts for the sake of others make a sannyāsi's actions unique and outstanding. Only a real sannyāsi can bring about a real change in others." In fact, sannyāsa, at least as a mental state, is the ultimate goal of spiritual life. It is for this alone the people of all the other āśramas [stages of life] are striving. It is the culmination of human life.

So, we can see that Amma's āśram has a place for everyone, as long as one has the maturity and dispassion to live a simple life, dedicated to spiritual progress. That said, not all of Amma's devotees need join the āśram. It may not suit one's current situation. It is a personal decision. More important than moving to Amṛtapuri is to make our homes themselves āśrams. Live your life, maintaining your family responsibilities and purifying your mind through putting Amma's teachings into practice. Treat all your family members as embodiments of God, and serve and love them accordingly. Such a home is verily an āśram. As Amma says,

---

[4] The Sannyāsi Saṅgha, as part of the 75th Anniversary of the Śrī Nārāyaṇa Guru Dharma Saṅgha Śivagiri Pilgrimage, on September 24, 2007, Śivagiri Maṭh, Varkkala, Tiruvanantapuram, Kerala.

"A true gṛhastāśrami is one who has made his *gṛham* [home] an āśram."

Amma stresses, time and time again, that more important than physical proximity is mental 'tuning.' Amma says, "Where there is love, there is no distance. The lotus may be millions of miles from the sun, but when the sun shines, its petals open nonetheless. On the contrary, even if you are sitting right next to a radio tower, if you have your radio tuned to the wrong frequency, you cannot enjoy the programs. The mosquito finds only blood in the udder of the cow, never milk."

One of Amma's gifts to us is the thousands of Amma Satsaṅg groups throughout the world. Through these centers, āśrams and devotee homes serving as meeting places, we can regularly spend time with fellow devotees, sing bhajans, chant divine names and engage in selfless-service projects. This will help us to maintain inspiration and enthusiasm with regards to our spiritual practices. It can also be a support system in times of personal trouble and turbulence. But we should remember that the satsaṅg groups are to help us orient our lives to *sat*—Truth—and not otherwise. They should be places we come for respite from worldly life—places of spiritual growth. Therefore we should leave all the gossip, worldly talk and competition at the door.

Furthermore everyone can—and lately it seems like everyone does—*visit* Amṛtapuri. Spending a few days, weeks or months in Amma's āśram is a wonderful way to gain inspiration and strengthen one's bond with Amma. Come, stay for a few weeks or months, recharge your spiritual battery and then take Amma and the āśram back home with you.

Chapter Five:

Purification Through Karma Yoga

"Selfless service is the soap that purifies our mind."

—Amma

AN IMPURITY IS a foreign element introduced into something that is otherwise homogenous. Whether on the physical or mental level, human beings cannot accept impurity. On the physical level, if the body develops a blemish, the hand will naturally go to that area and repeatedly try to remove it. It is the same on the mental level. Mental impurity mainly comes in the form of desire—our likes and dislikes. In its true pristine state, the mind is like the clear still surface of a lake—an all but transparent veil through which the bliss of the Self can clearly be experienced. Desires are like rocks dropped into this lake. The more intense the desire—the larger the rock—the more intense the mental disturbance. One way to quell the disturbance is to fulfill the desire. This is how the majority of people live, eternally chasing their likes and fleeing from their dislikes, never understanding the true psychological motivation spurring their actions, which is to simply experience peace.

Unfortunately, as Amma tells us, it is impossible to permanently uproot a desire through its fulfillment. When we remove the impurity of desire through fulfillment, the desire is quelled only temporarily. Sooner or later it comes back with more intensity, creating an even larger mental disturbance. The cycle is endless. Amma compares the phenomenon to scratching an itchy wound—temporarily one may feel some relief, but soon the itching starts up again, only this time it is worse due to infection. Or we can say that desire is like a bully, always pressuring us to give him money. If we buckle in, tomorrow he will only be back for more. If he asked for $20 the first time, the second time he will ask for $30. Instead of placating him, we should chase him away. Similarly, seeing the inherent flaw in trying to attain lasting peace through desire *fulfillment*, the scriptures tell us to go about it through desire *transcendence* instead.

Total transcendence of desire comes only with *mokṣa* [liberation]—the culmination of spiritual life, wherein one understands with doubtless conviction that 'I am not the body, emotions or intellect, but the ever-blissful and eternal consciousness that is the very core of my being.' Only this understanding can eradicate desire totally. This is because desire's root cause is ignorance regarding who we are. Identifying with the body, we fear injury and death. Identifying with the *prāṇa* [energy] within our body, we fear sickness. Identifying with the mind and its likes and dislikes, we become upset when the external arrangements do not live up to them. All this just because of a simple confusion regarding who we are. The body, emotional mind and intellect are all finite and limited entities. If we identify with them, it is only natural that we will feel finite, limited and incomplete as well. We then begin trying to rectify the situation. How do we do this? We look around, see certain things we don't have and think, 'Ah, if only I had *that*!' Thus, the vicious cycle begins. No external medication is going to cure the internal injury, though they may give temporary relief.

Although total transcendence can only take place through proper understanding regarding our true nature, this realization is a very subtle process. As such, it cannot take place in a mind perpetually disturbed by desires. It sounds like a no-win situation—as if the saints and sages are telling us, "You can never transcend desire without a peaceful mind." And when we ask how to attain that peaceful mind, they tell us "Transcend your desires." Is there any hope for us? This is where *karma yoga* comes in. Through karma yoga we can overcome our likes and dislikes to a great extent, making our minds more fit for the subtle process of Self-realization. This is the ultimate purpose of karma yoga. However, as we will see, the benefit of karma yoga is not only as a stepping-stone to Self-realization; karma yoga has some immediate perks of its own as well.

Karma yoga means 'the yoga of action.' It is a method of performing actions as a means to realizing our oneness with the *ātma*—the Self. However, in the Bhagavad-Gīta, Kṛṣṇa often refers to karma yoga as *buddhi yoga*—the yoga of the intellect. This is because it is not based upon a specific action but upon a specific mental attitude. Any action—from walking one's dog, to traditional *pūja,* to designing a bridge—when performed with the right attitude, is karma yoga. Conversely, even the most elaborate Vedic ritual or selfless service is mere action if not performed with the karma-yoga attitude.

Two members of the Opposing Party boarded a plane for a short flight to the capital. One took the window seat, the other the middle seat. Then, just before take-off, a member of the Ruling Party boarded and took the aisle seat. After takeoff, he kicked off his shoes, wiggled his toes and was just getting comfortable when the Opposition member in the window seat said, "I think I'll get up and get a Coke."

"No problem," said the Ruling Party member. "As a service to the country, I'll get it for you." As soon as he left, the Opposition member quickly picked up the man's right shoe and spat in it.

When the Ruling Party member returned with the Coke, the other Opposition member said, "Gee, that looks good. I think I'll have one too." Again, the Ruling Party member obligingly went to fetch it in the name of the country. And, sure enough, as soon as he left, the other shoe was promptly picked up and spat in. After he returned with the Coke, all three men tilted back their chairs and enjoyed the short flight.

When the flight was over, the Ruling Party member slipped his shoes back on and immediately realized what had happened. With a tinge of sadness in his voice, he said, "How long must this go on? This fighting between our parties? This hatred? This animosity? This spitting in shoes and urinating in Cokes?"

We can see from this joke that unless we are privy to the full situation, our understanding of an action is quite limited. Similarly, only when we know the mental attitude and true motivation with which an action has been performed can we determine whether or not it has been karma yoga.

As Amma always reminds us, results are dependent upon a vast latticework of factors, of which our own actions are but one. Accepting this reality, the karma yogi puts his focus on action and accepts with equanimity whatever results come. It is this attitude that Kṛṣṇa is advising Arjuna to adopt when he says:

karmaṇyevādhikāraste mā phaleṣu kadācana |

"Seek to perform your duty; but lay not claim to its fruits." [Bhagavad-Gīta, 2.47]

If we investigate, we'll see the undefeatable logic of this statement. Thereafter, living accordingly is not so much a spiritual outlook as it is mere 'street smarts.'

Let's take for an example being interviewed for a job. We can rehearse for the interview for weeks, having a friend ask us common questions and honing our answers. We have total control over what suit we choose, what color tie we pick. We can practice our smile in the mirror, work on developing a firm handshake, buy a $300 pair of shoes and get a $100 haircut. In the realm of action, we can plan and think and calculate as much as possible; more or less, we have complete control. Even after the interviewer poses his questions, we are still in control over what we say. However, as soon as we speak, we are no longer in control; the action has left us and become subject to the laws of cause-and-effect as dictated by the universal forces. The interviewer could be in a good mood or a bad mood based on previous interactions he's had that day. Our answers could trigger positive or negative memories in his mind. Anything can happen. When we leave his office, there is no point in worrying over the results, as we have no control over them. No matter how much we worry about how our answers were received, it will not change the interviewer's perceptions of us.

Once we understand that we have control over actions but not their results, we will stop worrying about results and shift our focus to perfection in action. Such a person is a karma yogi. He moves forward in life relatively unperturbed, peacefully abiding in the present moment.

KARMA YOGA ATTITUDES

One of the beautiful aspects of karma yoga is that it can be applied through various subtle variations. As long as its essence—'Do your best and accept the rest'—is undisturbed, we can modify our concept to suit our mindset. One popular attitude is to take God or guru as the master and ourselves as the servant. But one needn't even believe in God to perform karma yoga. As long as one accepts the fundamental laws of action—that we have control over our actions but not their results—even an atheist can perform karma yoga. As Amma says, "It doesn't matter if one believes in God or not as long as he or she properly serves society." As long as our attitude shifts our focus away from results and onto action, we will still receive the benefits associated with karma yoga. Within these parameters, we have liberty in selecting our concept.

We see that in Amma's childhood, she took all of her household chores as being done for Kṛṣṇa[1]. In this way, Amma performed all of her actions—sweeping, washing, cooking, tending to the cows, etc.—with tender love, care and devotion. I remember an incident several years ago when Amma helped a new *brahmacāri* [student disciple] to develop this attitude. One day during *darśan*, the brahmacāri told Amma all the various *sevas* in which he was currently engaged. As Amma herself had not specifically instructed him to do all of them, he wanted to make sure that they were sevas Amma, in fact, wanted him to do. He went up to Amma in the darśan queue and told her everything he was doing around the āśram. "Some of these jobs I've just picked up on my own," he told her. "Are they really things that Amma wants me to do?"

Amma answered in the affirmative and then, in order to drive the point home, said, "It is *I* who told you to do all those things."

After this darśan, he was able to see all of the jobs as having come directly from Amma herself and thus apply the proper attitude to his work.

The Bhagavad-Gīta stresses the karma-yoga attitude of seeing all our actions as *yajña*—an offering to God as an expression of gratitude for all he has bestowed upon us in life. If we think about it, God has given us so much, yet normally we just take it all for granted.

Our bodies, families, homes, minds, sense organs, even the entire universe, are all gifts with which God has blessed us. Performing our actions as yajña acknowledges this truth.

A devotee shared with me the following incident, which helps to illustrate this point. He'd recently had surgery and spent a week in the hospital. When he was discharged, he looked at his itemized

[1] Amma says that she had full understanding that her true nature was eternal blissful consciousness from birth itself. Therefore her motivation behind performing any spiritual practice—be it *karma yoga*, meditation or contemplation—was, and continues to be, only to serve as a demonstration to humankind and not for any benefit of her own.

bill. One of the charges—$1,500—was for oxygen. He told me, "Swāmiji, I never realized air was so expensive! I've been breathing air 24 hours a day for 60 years, yet God has yet to send me a bill!" What he said is correct. We've been living on this earth for our entire lives, yet God never sends us a rent bill. In fact all of the five elements—space, wind, fire, water, earth—are God's alone. Therefore in this second karma-yoga attitude, we acknowledge this reality and perform our actions as a small token of gratitude for all God is giving us.

Traditionally, a yajña is a form of worship in which one offers various oblations to the Lord—either by pouring them into a fire pit or by placing them at the feet of an idol or picture. When the yajña is finished, a portion of what was offered is taken as *prasād* [consecrated offering]. Through this attitude, we come to see our every action as such a yajña. Accordingly, we then see all the results of the actions we perform as God's prasād. In fact, Amma says, true worship of God is not limited to sitting in a pūja room, offering flowers to a picture or an idol for 20 minutes a day. One's entire life must become worship. The pūja-room worship is symbolic of how one's life should become. In pūja, everything is on a miniature scale. The all-pervasive, all-powerful Lord is reduced to a small idol. The offering of every deed is symbolized by the offering of flowers. A lifetime of worship is symbolized by our action with concentration and devotion for a few minutes. As Amma says, "Your heart is the real temple. It is there that you must install God. Good thoughts are the flowers to be offered to him. Good actions are the worship. Good words are the hymns. Love is the divine offering." When we see all we receive in life as God's prasād, there is no scope for stress, fear or agitation, etc., with regards to results. If we are able to see everything as God's prasād, we will never be depressed by what comes to us in life. We have peace in accepting: what I received was a precious gift from God, so is what I am receiving now and so too will be whatever I receive in the future.

An attitude suited for intellectually oriented spiritual seekers is to simply understand the necessity of transcending likes and dislikes in the grand scheme of Self-realization. Rationally accepting the logic behind this, the seeker shifts his focus from results to action simply in order to purify his mind of desires.

Another attitude Amma often mentions is considering ourselves not the performer of actions, but the instrument by which the actions are performed. Along these lines Amma says, "When performing actions, we should try to see ourselves as an instrument in the hands of God—like the pen in the hands of a writer or a brush in the hands of a painter. Our prayer should be 'O Lord, let me become a purer and purer instrument in your hands.'" An instrument does not have opinions and desires of its own; it only does what the one wielding it desires. If God is our wielder, then our only desire will be to live according to *dharma*—performing actions prescribed by our guru and the scriptures and avoiding those prohibited by them.

Whatever our attitude, if we are sincere we will immediately gain a relative amount of mental equanimity. This is why, when teaching Arjuna about karma yoga, Kṛṣṇa says: *samatvaṁ yoga ucyate*[2]—'[Karma] yoga is equanimity.' Because of his attitude, the mind of the karma yogi is no longer sprinting after or fleeing from sense objects. This puts him in a better position to see life more clearly—to reflect, assess and rationally analyze his experiences in life. When this happens, certain truths will become self-evident for him. Everywhere he looks, every time he acts, everywhere he goes, these truths will leap out at him. This experience will have a radical and irreversible impact upon his thinking.

THE NATURE OF OBJECTS

So what are some of these naked truths? First we will start to see that all attainments in this world are mixed with pain—in

[2] Bhagavad-Gīta, 2.48

attaining, maintaining and, of course, in losing. Secondly we will see that all objects have the potential to make us dependent upon them. And finally we will come to understand that no object gives true contentment. These are the three flaws in trying to find happiness through external objects.

In order to attain anything, some level of struggle is needed. The higher the attainment, the more difficult the struggle. Take for example becoming the elected leader of a country. Setting aside all the work needed just in order to become a candidate in the first place, you have to travel, make speeches, be patient and proper with everyone. In some countries you may have to hold debates, shake hands and even kiss babies. You also have to be careful of your every word and action because, if you make even the slightest slip-up, The Press and other candidates are ready to rip you to pieces. A man involved in politics recently told me that during a campaign many candidates even have to resort to taking pills in order to keep up with the grueling schedule! So, certainly there is struggle and pain in attaining. Then if you are lucky enough to be elected, you have to be even sharper: wars, economic problems, civil unrest, the budget... All your decisions will be analyzed and scrutinized, and the opposition is ever ready to impeach you. If you didn't get an ulcer during the election, certainly the struggle of maintaining the office will give you one. So there is pain in maintaining as well. And finally, when your term comes to an end and you have to step down from office—despite all the struggle—you are now depressed. It doesn't have to be a ministry or presidency, many times people feel it difficult to let go of their jobs when the time for retirement comes. They miss the sense of purpose their jobs gave them. So, certainly there is pain in losing as well.

The next truth we realize through our heightened level of introspection made possible through karma yoga is that nothing we attain ever makes us truly content. Don't we find that as soon as we get a raise, we start thinking about the next one? We first used to be satisfied with cassette players. After that it was CD players. Then mp3 CD players. Then it was iPod... iPod Touch... iPhone! Surely by the time this book comes out there will be something else entirely. There is nothing wrong with technology and scientific advancement. That is not the point. The point is that we always think that contentment is just around the corner—after we get our coffee, the raise, the wife, the child, the dream house, retirement... But this is an illusion. No object can provide us with eternal contentment.

I once read an essay by a man who had recently overcome an obsession with automobiles. He recounted how upon buying a certain car, he gave it a new paint job and painstakingly hand-rubbed it to a sheen. He then repeated the process. It looked even better. He did it again and definitely noticed an improvement. He decided to apply a third coat... a fourth... a fifth... a sixth... *Thirty-two* coats of paint later, the man finally realized he was heading down a bad path. There could be no end. With each coat of paint, the car shone more gloriously in the sun. He wondered, "If 32 coats of paint look this good, what would 132 look like?" He realized he had two options: dedicate his life to chasing the impossible or sell the car.

The awareness made possible through karma yoga helps us to realize the futility of attaining contentment through material pursuits and attainments. Some realize this after two coats of paint, others after 27, still others keep adding coats until their death—only to resume the quest in their next life.

Finally, karma yoga helps us to see that we can easily end up dependent upon any object—be it coffee, television, the Internet, mobile phones or pizza... It's truly as the saying goes, "First I owned it; then it owned me."

Once a guru was teaching his disciple about the nature of ownership. He said, "You may think you own a certain object or person. But at the same time, that object or person also owns you." Nearby there was a cowherd holding a calf by a rope. The guru walked over and freed the calf. The calf immediately bolted. Shocked, the cowherd ran after the cow. The guru said, "See? Who is tied to whom? The cow was tied to the cowherd by the rope, but the cowherd is tied to the cow by his attachment."

Of course, the most gross examples of this are drugs and alcohol. When people start drinking, they invariably end up losing their ability to be happy without it. But even relationships can become like this. How many times have we heard someone say after a breakup, "I just can't live without her!"

Once we see these inherent flaws in trying to obtain perfect happiness through the objects of the world, the objects naturally begin to lose their luster. In Vedānta, this understanding is called *vairāgya* [dispassion], and as we discussed in Chapter Three, it is an essential quality for one who hopes to attain Self-realization. How can we meditate, study the scriptures and engage in contemplation if our minds are infatuated with the objects of the world? Furthermore, unless we have dispassion for the objects of the world, we will never start seeking the true source of happiness. Only when we are fed up with the ephemeral, will we start a proper search for the eternal.

The awakening of this knowledge and its effect on the personality is beautifully illustrated in a *bhajan* Amma wrote called "Īśvarī Jagad-Īśvarī":

I have seen that this life of worldly pleasures is full of misery.
Don't make me suffer by making me like the moths
that fall into the fire...
What is seen today, tomorrow is not there.
Embodiment of consciousness, O your divine plays!
For that which truly exists, there is no destruction.
That which has destruction, doesn't really exist.
Please be kind and show the path to liberation, O eternal one!

As a spiritual aspirant, our vairāgya should be intense. In order to drive this point home, a 13th century saint named Sant Jñāneśvar wrote in his commentary upon the Bhagavad-Gīta that we should develop the same dispassion for sense pleasures as we would have toward using a python for a pillow, entering a tiger's den or leaping into a pit of molten iron. (Actually, these are the milder of his examples!) The idea is that, in this stage of spiritual life, one should not merely see sense pleasures as worthless, but as deadly.

According to the scriptures, proper vairāgya comes only when we are able to extend what we have learned regarding the flaws of sense objects we *have* experienced to all sense objects—even the ones we have *not* experienced. One shouldn't need to eat an entire bushel of red chilies to learn that all chilies are hot!

Once, a prince was crowned king. Upon his coronation, he immediately appointed his longtime friend, who was very intelligent, as his minister. The king's first instruction to him was to compile an almanac analyzing all of known history. The minister immediately set to work. Ten years later, he returned with a 50-volume set of books, intricately detailing and commenting upon all the known events that had taken place since the dawn of man. The king was in his pleasure garden at the time, the best musicians in the land serenading him and his queen. He took one look at the 50 volumes, winced and said, "It's too much. Can you please try to reduce it?"

The minister agreed and took leave of the king. Ten years later he returned, this time with a 10-volume set. But the king was again very busy, as an epidemic had recently struck the country, and he was fully engaged in remedying the situation. "Oh, I'm so busy!" he told the minister. "And still it is too long. Can't you reduce it further?"

Once again the minister agreed and took leave. Five years later, he returned again. This time he had just one book with him. "Here it is," he said. "One volume containing just the basic structure of human history." But recently there had been a clash between two groups of subjects, and the king was busy quelling the problem. He looked at the thick book and then back at his friend and said, "I apologize, but it is still too much. I just don't have time. Please try to reduce it further."

A year later, the minister finished the task. Somehow he had reduced the history to just one chapter. But when he reached the palace, he saw the king gearing up for battle, as a neighboring kingdom had begun encroaching upon their territory. "No time," the king said as he galloped away. "Try to reduce it more!"

A week later the minister made his way to the king's quarters, a mile or so behind the frontlines. There he found the king, lying in bed, dying from a mortal wound. The minister looked down at his dying friend—so frail and worn out from life—and said, "I did it, my lord. I reduced it to one page."

The king looked up at his minister and said, "I'm sorry, my good friend, but any moment now I will breathe my last. Please, quickly, before I die, give me the essence of what you have learned from all these years of study."

The minister nodded his head in agreement, and, with a tear in his eye, said, "People suffer."

History testifies to this truth. No one has ever attained anything without going through the pain of struggle. No sense object has ever provided anyone permanent contentment. And no one has ever derived happiness from any object without opening themselves up to the potential of becoming dependent upon it. Some of us learn these lessons quickly, others take lifetimes.

Many people think they will attain contentment through school, and it doesn't work. They then try for contentment through a career, and it doesn't work. They then try to attain contentment through marriage, and of course it doesn't work either. Thereafter many keep thinking it's only because they haven't found the *right* spouse! So they get married a second time... third time... fourth time. Some even move through all the different nationalities in this search—American spouse, Indian spouse, German spouse,

Japanese spouse... The saints and sages, tell us: 'Get married if you want but don't look for contentment there. There is nothing in all the three worlds that can bring it to you! For that you must turn within.'

As briefly mentioned in the previous chapter, overcoming our likes and dislikes is not about suppression. The saints and sages know that suppression never works. It only eventually results in a breakdown. Our transcendence has to come through right understanding—otherwise known as sublimation.

Once a novice spiritual aspirant approached his guru and confessed to him that he was having thoughts about ladies. Every time he sat to meditate, visions of various models and movie starlets would begin dancing in his head. He was really distraught. The guru listened quietly as the disciple lamented his plight, but he did not say anything. However the next day the guru called the disciple to him and handed him a small thin object wrapped in newspaper. He told the disciple to take it back to his room, open it and then put the object just to the left of the central idol on his altar. The disciple then took leave of the guru and followed his instructions. However when he unwrapped the object he saw that it was a picture of a beautiful and seductive-looking woman! He was shocked. He ran back to the guru and said, "What is this? I open my heart and confess a serious problem to you, and in return you mock me by giving me this photo! What's the deal here?" However the guru did not respond. He simply closed his eyes in meditation. The disciple was irritated, but eventually cooled down. After a while he thought, "Well, my guru is an enlightened master. He would not mislead me. Perhaps there is something to this." He then placed the picture on his altar next to the central idol.

Now when the disciple sat for his daily meditations, there were two 'gods' before him—the Infinite Lord and his movie star. More often that not, he found himself meditating upon the woman. He imagined traveling with her, joking with her, sharing his heart with her and marrying her. Each day was a new adventure, and he looked forward to his meditation sessions more and more.

But then one morning, as he and his new bride walked along the seashore in his mind, her attention was suddenly diverted by a handsome stranger! Soon the two were eloping, leaving our young disciple all alone. He tried to contact her, but she wouldn't take his calls. He was heartbroken and miserable. Finally she contacted him... with a summons for a divorce! He imagined the court-proceedings. She took him for everything he had. In the end he was left penniless, emotionally shattered and alone.

The disciple opened his eyes and came back to reality. When he did so, the two juxtaposed images on his altar stared back at him. Seeing the images side by side, he now understood the perfection and selflessness of divine love and the selfishness of worldly love. Realizing that, in giving him the photo, his master had not been mocking him but had actually been functioning at the deepest level of compassion, he ran to him and prostrated at his feet.

The guru did not want his disciple to *suppress* his thoughts about women. He wanted him to *transcend* them through understanding regarding the nature of worldly love. Having him place the photos side by side triggered the comparison and, eventually, the disciple's dispassion.

The disciple in the story was in fact of a high-caliber. He was able to develop dispassion through mere contemplation. There was no need for him to actually indulge his desire. However many are not at this level. When desires come, one should try to negate them using one's power of discriminative thinking. But if they continue to pester us, we may have to indulge them. As long as they fall in line with dharma, there is nothing wrong in this. But when indulging one's desires, one should maintain awareness, try to see the desired object's limitations and, thereby, gain the mental strength to transcend it. When our understanding is clear, our infatuation with the comforts and pleasures of the world will naturally come to an end. As Amma says, "You don't bathe in a river forever; you bathe in it to come out fresh and clean."

Along these lines, there is a verse from Muṇḍaka Upaniṣad that says:

parīkṣya lokān karma-citān
brāhmaṇo nirvedamāyāstyakṛtaḥ kṛtena |

"After examining and seeing the defects of all that can be acquired through action, understanding the truth that nothing eternal can be attained by action, a wise person should renounce action[3]." [Muṇḍaka 1.2.12]

Thus, until we get the clarity, the saints tell us to test out the world. Go out there and examine the pleasures and comforts of the world, see what it has to offer you. Experience for yourself. But once you see the defects in obtaining happiness from the world, understand that everything out there has the same defects. No need to test them all. So, thereafter, stop performing actions in order to obtain happiness and instead seek to realize the Self—the true source of all bliss. Thereafter actions will still be performed (we still have to eat, don't we?), but we sever the connection in our mind between action and happiness. We then move from selfish actions to selfless ones.

KARMA YOGA PERKS

Dispassion toward the attainments and objects of the world and stoking the fire of our pursuit of the Self is the primary aim of karma yoga. But as mentioned earlier in this chapter, karma yoga has some perks of its own. It is an advantageous attitude for even a so-called 'non-spiritual' person to adopt.

[3] Here, 'action' indicates selfish actions, not selfless actions performed to purify the mind as part of the spiritual path.

The first perk of karma yoga is that it heperklps us to actually perform our actions better. Take the example of the job interview with which we began the chapter. Understanding that he has control only over action and not the results, the karma yogi's concentration is not split. It is 100 percent focused on the action—in this case, listening to, thinking over and answering the questions. Obviously a person with undivided attention will perform at a higher standard than one whose attention is divided. Worrying over how his answer to the interviewer's first question was perceived, the non-karma yogi will not be able to focus properly on his second question.

Nowhere has this concept picked up more acceptance than in the world of sports. In 2000, a sports psychologist named H.A. Dorfman wrote a book called *The Mental ABC's of Pitching: A Handbook for Performance Enhancement*, which has been read and praised by professional baseball pitchers. Dorfman writes that when pitching one should only think of three things: pitch selection, location and the catcher's mitt, his target[4]. If he finds other thoughts entering his mind, he should stop and take a moment to get his head right before continuing. In the end, Dorfman concludes that a pitcher shouldn't judge his performance by how well the batters he faced hit his pitches, but instead by whether or not he threw the pitches he wanted to throw.

Why do people 'choke' in sports? Because they are focused on the possibility of losing. Most of us can remember some situation in our childhood where we were playing a game and the final crucial play of the game all came down to us... and we panicked and blew it. Basketball offers one of the best examples. If a player is fouled in basketball, he often gets a chance to take two free throws. For a professional basketball player, a free throw is relatively easy. He gets to take two 15-foot shots, facing the basket square on, with no one defending it. The average for the NBA

[4] In cricket, this would be ball selection, line and length, and the stumps.

[National Basketball Association] is approximately 75 percent. But what about in high-pressure situations? For example, the final two minutes of a game, with neither team ahead by more than three points. The pressure is felt much more. Why? It is the exact same shot; there should be no difference. But if we allow the mind to focus on the importance of making the shot, rather than the shot itself, our performance will suffer. According to statistics, the NBA average (2003 – 2006) falls by 2.3 percent in such 'clutch' situations as specified above. In short, we perform better when we focus on action, not on results.

This is not to say we shouldn't pay attention to results. When the results come, we should evaluate them calmly and logically. Based on our evaluation—what went wrong, what went right, etc.—we can then adjust our actions accordingly the next time.

Another benefit of karma yoga is that it actually helps one to enjoy life. We are, more or less, constantly engaged in action. However the prime results of those actions only come occasionally. If we focus on the action, we can enjoy the action itself—the peace and joy of a mind merged in its job. Take washing the dishes. If our mental focus is fixated on having all the dishes clean and dry and back in the cupboard, we will only experience joy when the final clean and dry dish is resting back in its proper place. However if we focus on the action, we enjoy the entire duration of the job. I am sure this is something we have all noticed. If we are focused on finishing, the job is a chore. If we surrender to the moment, it becomes a blissful experience—be it washing the dishes, digging a trench or ironing the clothes.

Along these lines, it is worth noting that even to enjoy the sense objects life has to offer us, we need to cultivate at least a relative amount of control over our desires. Otherwise, while trying to enjoy one sense object, the desire for another may divert our focus and somewhat spoil the intensity of our enjoyment. Suppose you are enjoying a wedding feast. All your favorite dishes are laid out for you: rice, *sāmbār*, *dāl*, various delicious curries, different types of pickle, banana chips, pudding, etc. You start eating and immediately are transported to sense-pleasure heaven! But suddenly you realize you have run out of chickpea curry. You continue to eat, but your mind is now divided. Part of it is focused on locating the waiter carrying around the second servings of chickpea curry. You still enjoy the food in front of you, but not as wholeheartedly as you would if you were 100 percent focused upon it.

When I first joined the *āśram*, there were only a handful of us. Except when Amma was giving darśan we more or less had her all to ourselves. In light of the thousands upon thousands of people who come for Amma's darśan today, it is quite hard to imagine. We could sit next to Amma hour after hour and talk to her freely without ever having to consider others' desire to do so. I remember once during Devi Bhāva, Amma called me to her side. She began talking to me about various things, answering my questions and generally showering me with affection. At one point she laid my head down on her lap, allowing me to lie like that as she continued to give darśan. I think I stayed like that for more than an hour! Externally could there be any higher heaven? There was one problem though: after about 30 minutes, when another brahmacāri started playing the *tabala* [drums], I realized it was supposed to be my turn! Back then I had a real passion for playing the tabala. I was just beginning to play, and as such my enthusiasm was very high. This other brahmacāri and I would take turns. (There may have been some *slight* competition between us as well.) With my head resting in Amma's lap, I thought, "What an arrogant fellow! He knows it's my turn to play! He should have come here and asked me for permission to take my turn." Soon, even though my head was lying in the most peaceful place in the world, my mind was completely focused on this other brahmacāri and his tabala playing! As I listened to him play, I imagined that the sound was actually me playing tabala—hard on his *head*! Of course, Amma knew what I was thinking. As soon as the bhajan session was finished, Amma told me to get up and let someone else sit with her. Due to my intense desire to play the tabala, I lost both the chance to play as well as the chance to fully enjoy being in Amma's presence. Now, I can confidently say that no one's tabala playing could make me jealous, but today there is no opportunity to rest my head on Amma's lap for one hour!

This is why Amma says that the real hell is not a physical plane but a state of mind. So, too, heaven. A mind truly purified of its likes and dislikes can be happy anywhere—be it a physical hell or a physical heaven. Similarly, a mind full of unfulfilled desires can be in hell even in a physical heaven.

In the Gīta there is a famous verse presenting yet another karma-yoga perk:

nehābhikramanāśo'sti pratyavāyo na vidyate |

"In karma yoga no effort is ever wasted; nor is there any harmful effect." [Bhagavad-Gīta, 2.40]

The idea is that if we fail in an action performed with the karma-yoga attitude, there is no loss because we will learn from our mistakes and gain in mental purification. However, if we fail in actions in which our primary focus is the result, then the loss is total. Just imagine a writer who spends years writing and editing a book only to find no one is interested in publishing it. If his sole focus was becoming a famous best-selling novelist, his loss is total. He feels totally frustrated, as he watches all his years of efforts swirling down the drain. And in the depression of his failure, he doesn't even learn anything. However if he had written the book with the karma-yoga attitude, he would have learned so much about writing, publishing, human nature and himself in general.

Not only does performing work as karma yoga benefit the individual, it also benefits society as a whole. Because the karma yogi is always aiming at perfection in action, he always does his work to the best of his abilities. Unfortunately, more often than not, the prevailing work-place attitude today is: 'Do the minimum, get the maximum.'

Along these lines, someone once shared with me a list of tricks for looking busy while, in fact, doing almost nothing. My three favorites were: 1) Never clean your desk, as an untidy desktop makes the impression that you don't have a spare second to waste on things as insignificant as cleanliness. 2) If you wear glasses, leave an old pair on the desk as though you will be right back. Then go home. 3) Buy a neck brace, paint it the color of your skin and sleep at your desk while sitting up.

People who are focused only on a paycheck will constantly cut corners, sleep on the clock and goof off in general. If possible, they will come in late, extend their lunch breaks and leave 30 minutes early. This is what we generally see when we look around many offices.

It was the karma-yoga attitude that set the Āśram's tsunami-relief work apart from that done by the government. In the end, the Āśram was the first organization in India to complete tsunami-relief houses built according to government standards. I remember Amma once commenting on the speed of work done by the Āśram: "The brahmacāris worked day and night," she said. "Amma would often call the brahmacāri in charge and ask him how the work was going, and no matter what hour Amma would call, he would be there working—midnight, two a.m., four a.m. Will it be like this with paid workers? No, they work only eight hours a day, stopping three times to eat and two more to drink tea."

Imagine if our entire planet adopted the karma-yoga attitude with regards to their work. Imagine a world where people not only worked for salary but also because they saw all their actions as worship. How productive and efficient the world would become!

Finally, even if we discount the fact that it is a crucial step in transcending all suffering, via Self-realization, karma yoga also prevents us from suffering prior to enlightenment. To understand this, it is helpful to look at another verse in the Gīta, wherein Kṛṣṇa explains why people persist in engaging in sinful actions despite understanding that it is unwise to do so:

kāma eṣa krodha eṣa rajoguṇa samudbhavaḥ |
mahā-śano mahā-pāpmā viddhyenam-iha-vairiṇam ||

"It is desire and anger rising from mental agitation; know this to be insatiable, the root of all sin and the greatest enemy in this world." [Bhagavad-Gīta, 3.37]

When intense enough, desires can pressure us to act in a selfish fashion even at the expense of the happiness and harmony of our fellow man. According to the law of karma, such actions come back to us sooner or later in the form of negative experiences. In fact all the adverse circumstances and painful situations we are currently experiencing are the result of some selfish action performed in our past—either in this life or before. Why did we perform these selfish actions? Because our desires got out of control. Through karma yoga our desires are, at the least, kept in check, as we gain the control to always follow dharma. In this way, we are setting our self along a path in which we will reap only good karma in the future.

From these examples we can see that applying the karma-yoga attitude not only purifies our mind, making it ready for the process of Self-realization, but also has a lot of benefits in the here-and-now: helping us to love life, learn from life and give back to life more than ever before.

Although all of our actions can (and in the case of a spiritual seeker, must) be performed with the karma-yoga attitude, Amma stresses the importance of applying this attitude with regard to seva—selfless service. In fact, actions can be broadly classified into three categories: *niṣkāma*, *sakāma* and *niṣiddha*—respectively, these are selfless actions, actions born out of our personal likes and dislikes, and actions forbidden due to the fact they are harmful to ourselves, society and Nature. Obviously, once we understand an action is forbidden, we should stop engaging in it. Otherwise we are sure to eventually reap its negative fruit. But a spiritual seeker should not only abstain from forbidden actions, he should also gradually try to decrease selfish actions and replace them with selfless ones.

For a novice, Amma recommends that we begin by spending just 30 minutes a day working for the benefit of others. Whether it is volunteering somewhere or simply donating a portion of our salary, this will get us moving in the right direction. From there, we can gradually, when possible, try to increase the amount of selfless actions we perform. In this way, 30 minutes can mark the beginning of a gradual transformation. Many people find that they eventually develop a fondness for such work and then, upon their retirement, instead of just enjoying the fruit of their life's labors, they continue to work for the uplift of others. Our selfish desires are gradually replaced with the desire to purify our minds or the desire to help the world. Unlike selfish desires, such desires are the means to liberation. They are not drawbacks for a seeker, but assets to be sought and cultivated. These are the desires that help us to overcome all other desires.

Chapter Six:

Expanding Our Vision

"We should try to see everyone as God."

—Amma

AS PART OF karma yoga, the scriptures speak of five forms of worship that everyone should perform throughout their lives. These are called the *pañca mahā-yajñas*—the five great forms of worship. Whether we are aware of it or not, through the social and spiritual activities undertaken by the Āśram, Amma is in fact leading us in accordance with these ancient mind-expanding traditions, all of which are ideal forums for applying the karma-yoga attitude.

The first yajña is called Brahma Yajña (sometimes referred to as Ṛṣi Yajña). It is an expression of gratitude toward all the ancient sages who have shown us the path to freedom from sorrow. This is done by learning and propagating the teachings of our guru and the scriptures. Amma says, "One of the ways to express our gratitude to *mahātmas* is by practicing what they have taught us and passing on this knowledge to others." In fact mahātmas like Amma don't desire our worship or gratitude. Having realized total fulfillment in the Self, they are complete as is. Brahma Yajña benefits the worshipper, society and all of creation. The one who studies the scriptures learns all about life and how to live in a harmonious fashion with his fellow beings and Nature. Furthermore when we share what we have learned with others, we fulfill their birthright to such knowledge as well. If everyone allowed their spiritual wisdom to die with them, there would be no hope for future generations.

Obviously, as Amma's children, we are all regularly engaging in this yajña. We listen to Amma's talks, read her books and try to put her teachings into practice. Even though one should await the guru's instruction before giving public talks, we can all share how Amma has helped our lives with those who ask. This is all Brahma Yajña.

Deva Yajña is worship of God. All of our chanting of *mantras*, meditation, singing *bhajans*, etc, fall under this yajña. Yet specifically this yajña is worshipping God in the form of the five elements and natural forces. According to the scriptures, all of the natural forces and elements are pervaded with consciousness, and are thus said to be presided over by specific *devatas* [demigods]. The entire creation is taken as the physical body of the Lord, and honored, respected and worshipped. As Amma mentioned in a speech she delivered in Paris in 2007, *Compassion: The Only Way to Peace*, "In the old days, there was no specific need for environmental preservation because protecting Nature was part of worshipping God and life itself. More than remembering 'God,' the people used to love and serve Nature and society. They saw the Creator through the creation. They loved, worshiped and protected Nature as the visible form of God." When we see the wind, rain, sun and earth, etc. as manifestations of God, we will naturally respect and honor them. No one who truly sees a river as Varuṇa Deva [the god of the water] could dump toxic waste into it.

For many years now during the *pūja* Amma leads before Devi Bhāva, she always asks us to pray for world peace, saying that Mother Nature is agitated and only the cool breeze of God's grace can dispel the gathering dark clouds. Amma says that Nature is disturbed because people are not living in harmony with the world around them. If we look at all the natural disasters in the world today, we will see that they are direct outcomes of man's exploitation of Nature. Amma points out that Mother Nature is reacting and destroying humanity with the very elements that are supposed to help us prosper. The winds that are supposed to cool us and spread seeds and rain, come to us instead as hurricanes and tornados. The sun that is supposed to warm us is melting the polar caps. The water that bathed and nourished us is instead withdrawing from our wells and smashing us with tsunami waves. The very earth that supports all is shaking with earthquakes.

Pitṛ Yajña is paying respect to and remembering one's deceased forefathers—without whom one would not have even been able to take birth. However, we can take this yajña as a reminder to respect and honor all our living senior relatives and elders as well. After all the scriptures tell us:

mātṛdevo bhava | pitṛdevo bhava |

"May mother be God to you. May father be God to you." [Taittirīya Upaniṣad, 1.11.2]

What is the point of worshipping our departed grandparents if we are then going to verbally abuse and disrespect our living parents? Amma says, "Expressing gratitude to our ancestors for the love and care they gave us sets an example to our children. Witnessing us loving and honoring our parents, our children, in turn, will love and honor us as well."

Amma always tells children that before they leave the house on some errand, they should pay their respects to their elders. In India this means bowing down and touching their feet, but in other cultures it can take on other forms. In general, children should make it a habit to take leave of their parents before going to school, etc. In Amma's schools, every year they have a day where all the mothers gather for their children to perform their *pāda-pūja*—reverential washing of the feet. We cannot underestimate the impact such rituals have on the minds of children (and parents), helping them to see the divine in every aspect of creation. We are ultimately trying to live with the understanding that the entire creation is God embodied. What better place to begin this than with our parents, who in at least a relative sense are our creators and sustainers? Unfortunately, these days many people are not following this teaching. As soon as their parents get old, they send them off to the nursing home—perhaps visiting them once a month for an hour or so. It seems a long way from following the Vedic proclamation of seeing them as God.

The fourth yajña is Bhūta Yajña, which is taking care of plants and animals, etc., seeing them as divine. In this regard, it is worth reflecting upon just how dependent we are on the flora and fauna with whom we share this earth. Without plant and animal life, humans would have nothing to eat. Even the maintenance of oxygen is only possible due to carbon-dioxide's conversion by the plant kingdom.

Amma often speaks about the environmental peril currently facing the planet. Along these lines, she explains how chemical fertilizers are destroying the honeybee population. Amma reminds everyone, "Bees play a vital role in the preservation of Nature and society. They pollinate the plants that provide us with fruit and grains. Similarly, humankind benefits from each and every living creature. All beings on earth depend on one another for survival. If the engine of a plane is damaged, it cannot fly. But even if just a single vital screw is damaged, the plane also cannot fly. Similarly, even the tiniest living being plays an important role. All living creatures need our help as well in order to survive. They are also our responsibility."

Finally there is Manuṣya Yajña, sometimes referred to as Nṛu Yajña. This is honoring and respecting our fellow human beings as embodiments of God. Traditionally, one of the ways this yajña was performed was by offering food and clothing to any unexpected guest who happened to come to the house, particularly those on religious pilgrimages who needed a place to stay for the night. Throughout India, we still see an unparalleled openness and warm-heartedness toward guests. It's something that many foreigners comment upon when visiting the country. With regards to Manuṣya Yajña, it is worth contemplating how indebted we are to our fellow man for everything from the food that finds its way to our tables to the electricity that illumines our homes, to the shoes we wear on our feet.

Of all the five yajñas, I would say Amma is putting the most stress on Manuṣya Yajña. Amma says, "It is Amma's wish that all of her children should dedicate their lives to spreading love and peace throughout the world. Real love and devotion for God is to have compassion for the poor and the suffering. My children, feed those who are hungry, help the poor, console the sorrowful, comfort the suffering, be charitable to all." On Amma's birthday, she always says that, rather than wash Amma's feet, she would be happier if her devotees were to engage in service to the poor. And this is exactly what is taking place. The Āśram's orphanage, hospitals, homes-for-the-homeless project, pension program, disaster-relief, hospices, scholarships for the poor... all are forms of Manuṣya Yajña.

WHEN WE PERFORM such yajñas, it is important to remember what makes them different from mere service. This is the understanding that we are worshipping God. As Ramaṇa Maharṣi wrote in his treatise Upadeśa Sāram:

> jagata īśadhī yukta-sevanam |
> aṣṭa-mūrti-bhṛd-deva-pūjanam ||

> *"Serving the world with the attitude of serving the Lord is (the true) worship of God, who is the wielder of the eight-fold forms."* [Upadeśa Sāram, 5]

The 'eight-fold forms' are the five elements (space, wind, fire, water and earth), the sun, the moon and all beings. Thus, it is not that we are helping our fellow man and plants and animals because God *wants* us to, but because we understand that they *are* God. This is the meaning behind the statement: *nāra seva nārāyaṇa seva*—'Service to man is service to God.' Similarly we understand the rivers, animals and trees are also manifestations of God[1]. So, too, our parents. This is important because it is this attitude that helps our actions bring about not only purification of mind but also expansion of mind—the gradual destruction of the limitations we place upon our concepts regarding what the world is and what God is.

Here is an example of how this works with regard to Bhūta Yajña—worship of God through protection of flora and fauna. In some of Amma's schools, a form of Bhūta Yajña has been initiated wherein the teachers have each child plant a sapling, give it a name and worship it through daily watering. From this, the teachers report something very beautiful. They say that when vacation time comes, many children go to their plants and say to them, "Oh, during vacation, I won't be here to water you. But don't be sad. I will come back in two months. Don't cry." No one has told the children to talk this way to their saplings; they just do it naturally. From naming their plants and watering them daily, they have spontaneously developed a relationship with them. Some children have even written letters and hung them on their saplings, telling them, "When you are sad, just read my letter." Now throughout these children's lives, they will have the understanding that trees are not inert objects but are sentient and have feelings. The vision of these children regarding the world they live in has begun expanding. Ultimately they can come to understand that the entire universe is pulsating with divinity—the

---

[1] According to Ādi Śaṅkarācārya's commentary on Viṣṇu Sahasranāma, the word *nārāyaṇa* itself invokes this truth. *Nara* means *ātma* [Self]; therefore (according to Sanskrit grammar) *nāra* means 'the effects of ātma'—i.e. the five elements that comprise the universe. *Ayana* means 'abode.' Therefore nārāyaṇa means 'the one whose abode is the five great elements.'

universe within and the universe without. If performed with the right mindset, the pañca mahā-yajñas can ultimately help us to see our Self in others and others in our Self. And in this understanding lies real transcendence.

Chapter Seven:

Cultivating Divine Qualities

"Children, God has given us the necessary faculties to become like him. Love, beauty and all divine qualities exist within us. We should make use of our faculties to express these divine qualities in our lives."

—Amma

EVERY RELIGION STRESSES the importance of cultivating good qualities—being kind, telling the truth, not stealing, etc. In short, we should follow the Golden Rule of 'Do unto others as you would have them do unto you.' In one form or another, this expression is found in the sacred books of all the world's religions, including Hinduism, wherein during Bṛhaspati's education of Yudhiṣṭhira in the Mahābhārata, the *guru* of the *devatas* [demigods] says:

na tat parasya saṁdadhyāt pratikūlaṁ yadātmanaḥ |
eṣa saṁkṣepato dharmaḥ kāmādanya pravartate ||

"One should never do that to another which one would regard as injurious to one's own self. This, in brief, is the rule of dharma. Other behavior is due to selfish desires."
[Mahābhārata, 13.114.8]

Character refinement not only plays a role in establishing social harmony but also in establishing the harmony of the individual. In fact, the scriptures again and again say that without refining one's character, a spiritual seeker can have no hope of Self-realization:

> nāvirato duścaritānnāśānto nāsamāhitaḥ |
> nāśantamānaso vā'pi prajñānen-ainam-āpnuyāt ||

> *"One who has not desisted from bad conduct, whose senses are not under control, whose mind is not concentrated, whose mind is not free from anxiety, cannot attain this Self through knowledge."* [Kaṭha Upaniṣad, 1.2.24]

The scriptures enumerate seemingly countless qualities to be cultivated. This is due to the exhaustive exploration of the human persona—in all its subtle facets—undertaken by the saints and sages. The voluminous lexicon of Sanskrit is a testament to just how precise and thorough the great intellects of ancient India were. How many dozens of words for 'sorrow' are enumerated—all reflecting subtle variations of grief. How many different types of pride are detailed! How many types of love! The great intellects of those times even divided the human smile into six distinct variations. In the 13th chapter of the Bhagavad-Gīta alone, Śrī Kṛṣṇa enumerates more than 20 qualities a sincere seeker should develop.

In this chapter, we will focus on some of the virtues to which Amma gives special prominence—namely, the cultivation of patience, innocence, humility, awareness and compassion. While these and other qualities are universal, we find that different scriptures and different gurus each stress certain qualities more than others. Perhaps this is due to the needs of the times or to the particular mindset of their devotees and disciples. Whatever the case may be, Amma says that in the beginning it is enough if we just focus on developing one good quality: "Just pick one quality and observe it with utmost faith and optimism; other qualities will automatically follow."

In order to illustrate this point, Amma tells the story of a woman who wins a beautiful crystal chandelier as first prize in a competition. She takes it home and hangs it in her living room. Enjoying its beauty, she suddenly notices that the paint on her living-room walls has faded and looks dirty in contrast with the new shining chandelier. She then decides to give the walls a fresh paint job. When she finishes that, she looks at the room and notices the curtains are dirty. This inspires her to take all the curtains down and give them a good wash. She then notices that the rug on the floor has become totally thread-bare. So she removes that and replaces it with a new one. Finally the room looks completely new. What in the end resulted in a complete transformation of the house, all began with just one small change—the new chandelier.

Or we can think about this concept of Amma's in terms of physical refinement. Let's say a man realizes he's out of shape and wants to do some physical exercise. So he decides to do some push-ups. Every day he gets down on the floor and does as many as he can. After a month or so, he really feels different, and when he looks in the mirror he sees how much stronger his chest and shoulders look. But then, in comparison, his biceps look small. So he gets some hand weights and adds a set of curls into his workout. After that he wants to improve his stomach, so he begins doing sit-ups. Then it's squats to build his legs... A year later we can't even recognize the guy. He's become an Arnold Schwarzenegger!

Such development is due to an expansion in awareness. We cultivate one good quality and suddenly, in our minds, it italicizes our negative qualities. Before, even though we knew the negative qualities were there, we did not care much because they did not force us to look at them very often. They were in plain view for *other* people—our family, friends and co-workers—but, due to our lack of awareness, were hidden from us.

In the scriptures, positive qualities are referred to as *daivi sampat*—divine[1] qualities, whereas negative qualities are referred to as *āsuri sampat*—demonic qualities. Inherently, we are neither good nor evil; we are the substratum of consciousness upon which such dualities manifest. But as the mind is matter, it will assume one quality or the other. Where there is no day, there can only be night. Generally, where virtue is absent, only its opposite will be found. For example, if one is not compassionate, what can one be but apathetic? If one is not humble, he must be egoistic. If one is not patient, he must be impatient. The quality of our mind is in our control. We can either allow it to deteriorate into the stuff of demons or we can refine it until it shines with the glories of the gods.

This concept is reflected in the ancient legends of India, wherin a sage named Kaśyapa had two wives: Aditi and Diti. Aditi gave birth to *ādityas* [demigods] and Diti gave birth to *daityas* [demons]. This allegory symbolizes how one individual is capable of good or evil depending upon his mind.

Just because a quality—be it godly or demonic—does not have the occasion to express itself does not mean it does not exist within a given individual's psyche. Certainly one end of the spectrum exists in his subconscious and, when the proper occasion occurs, will manifest. A king who is waited on hand and foot may not have many occasions to express patience or impatience. But keep him waiting for dinner and we will see what comes to the surface. So too, a monk living alone in a cave may not have much opportunity to express compassion or apathy, yet within him one of those two qualities is predominant. A *mahātma* will naturally manifest only godly qualities, for he has transcended all selfish likes and dislikes and will act seeing all as extensions of his own Self. Furthermore he will follow the dictates of dharma in order to set an example to others. The actions of an ordinary

[1] They are 'divine' because their cultivation helps us progress toward realizing our divine nature.

person will depend upon the strength of his attachment to his likes and dislikes versus the power of his attachment to dharma. It's like we have a balance-scale—with attachment to likes and dislikes on one side and attachment to dharma on the other. If the former is more powerful, we will behave like a devil; if the latter, a god. If one sets off to meditate in isolation prior to overcoming his likes and dislikes, he may come to think he has transcended them simply due to the lack of stimulus to trigger their outward symptoms. Only when we are made aware of our negative qualities can we set about putting forth the effort to transform them into positive ones.

Someone has told me there is a good demonstration of this principle in an animated children's movie called *Finding Nemo.* In the film, there is a group of sharks who've decided to stop eating fish. They've even formed a group called 'Fish Eaters Anonymous.' During their meeting they remind each other over and over again that "Fish are friends—not food!" The leader of the group is a huge Great White Shark, who proudly proclaims that it has been three weeks since his last fish. Everything seems to be going well for the sharks, until a fish swimming nearby happens to cut himself and a tiny drop of blood slowly begins floating up toward the leader shark's nose. Of course the second he smells the blood, his fish *vāsana* [tendency] is awakened and, suddenly, there is no containing him. He becomes a veritable madman, chasing the fish all over the ocean in attempts to devour it.

By this example, I don't mean to say that we need to dangle tempting sense objects before us, but neither can we hide from them forever. In the beginning of spiritual life, it is important to engage in *dama* [sense control] and avoid the presence of tempting sense objects. But eventually we need to become strong enough to transcend the need for such isolation. As Amma says, "A plant should be protected by a fence until it has grown big. After that, there is no problem." Only when we can stand face to face with a sense object, without feeling even a flicker of desire for it, can the vāsana be said to be truly eradicated.

Demonic qualities manifest when we identify with something limited—i.e. the body or mind. Godly qualities come when we identify with something unlimited—consciousness. Thus the more we are identified with our body and mind, the more demonic our nature will be. The more identified we are with the Self, the more godly. The ultimate nature of the Self is beyond all such dualistic concepts like good and bad, but in order to realize this reality, we must first purify our minds through the cultivation of divine qualities. In this way, righteous and good behavior becomes like a stepping stone, making the transition from selfishness to selflessness possible.

Let us now look at those divine qualities to which Amma gives prominence and examine some ways we can go about cultivating them. Remember, just because Amma stresses these qualities does not mean she considers other divine qualities unimportant and that we can ignore them.

PATIENCE

Amma says that patience is a quality that is needed from beginning to end in spiritual life. "Spiritual life is possible only for someone with a lot of patience," Amma says. "Otherwise only disappointment will be the result." In the modern age, everyone wants the fruit of their actions without any delay whatsoever. Today, almost all advertising contains the word 'instant'—*instant* loans, *instant* messaging, *instant* credit reports, *instant* results... People even speak of 'instant enlightenment.' Amma says the need for speed is becoming like a sickness. Anything of value takes time to cultivate. We are even seeing this with regard to the vegetables being produced today. Through new farming technologies, agricultural scientists have been able to reduce the time from seed to harvest, but the resulting vegetables contain less nutritional value.

I have heard a joke. A man prays to God: "Please, God, give me patience—*right now*." Unfortunately it does not work like this. In many ways, spiritual growth is like the blossoming of a flower. It is a gradual process that takes care and patience. One cannot break open the seed and pull out the sprout. One cannot force open the petals. Unfortunately, in the modern age, people demand spiritual upliftment as fast as possible. Amma says, "This is like a mother saying to her baby, 'I want you to grow up right now! Why must you keep being a child for so long? Hurry up! I don't have time to wait!' What would you say about such a mother, except that she is either extremely foolish or deranged? People expect a miracle to happen. They have no patience to wait or to make any effort. They don't understand that the real miracle consists of the opening up of one's heart into the one supreme truth. That inner blossoming, however, is always slow and steady."

If we don't have patience, we can never hope to progress in spiritual life. For decades we have been allowing the mind to do whatever it pleases. Now, suddenly, we are trying to assert control. We have been living for material results, now we are trying to go beyond such short-sightedness. We are trying to replace negativities with values, hatred with love, apathy with compassion. For most of us, our vāsanas are deeply rooted and to uproot them will take dedication and sincerity. Before the culmination of spiritual life, we have to utterly reverse our way of thinking about ourselves, about the world around us, even about God. This is not something that can take place overnight.

INNOCENCE

Perhaps Amma speaks about the importance of cultivating innocence more than any other quality. In its ultimate sense, Amma means 'innocence' as verily the fruit of Self-knowledge—an ever-fresh and blissful perspective regarding everything one perceives. But on a more relative level, Amma uses the word innocence to mean the cultivation of childlike faith and receptivity—the attitude of a beginner. Without these qualities, one will never be able to grow. Without faith in our guru and scriptures, we won't even be able to start on the spiritual path. Without receptivity, we will reject everything that doesn't fit into our current perspective. And without the attitude of a beginner, we will quickly become frustrated and give up. These qualities help us see life through the eyes of a child—with at least some degree of wonder and joy. This will enrich our lives as well as the lives of others.

"If we always have the attitude of a beginner, every situation will be an opportunity for us to learn," Amma says. "A beginner is always ignorant and he knows that he is ignorant. Therefore, he listens intently. He is open and receptive. Once you think that you know, then you do not listen anymore; you only speak. Your mind is already full."

Being a beginner doesn't mean that we don't make any progress or that we have to continually forget everything we've learned. It means retaining total openness, attentiveness and receptivity. Amma says that this is the only way to truly imbibe knowledge and wisdom.

In his innocence, a child is ever ready to forgive and forget. In fact, he doesn't even think about it as 'forgiveness.' It is automatic. But we are just the opposite. We cling to grudges and slights for years—even lifetimes. Amma says some people even pray that they are able to come back in another life in order to take further revenge against people who've wronged them. On the other hand, children may get upset with one another one minute and are happily playing together once again the next. Amma says this is the type of mind we should cultivate—a mind capable of forgiving and forgetting.

In innocence we are open and receptive and full of faith. If you tell a child he is a king with magic powers, he will immediately accept it. In spiritual life, the guru tells us all types of things about our true nature and the true nature of the world around us—much of which we have a hard time swallowing. At such times, we would definitely benefit from a little bit of the child of our youth.

There's an incident that took place many years ago that clearly illustrates this point. One night, one of the āśramites was up late lying on his bed, thinking of Amma. Suddenly he happened to see a mosquito heading toward his forehead. Believing it was Amma coming to bless him in the form of a mosquito, he allowed it to bite him, making sure not to move or disturb it as it sucked his blood. The mosquito ended up leaving a big welt where it had bitten him—exactly in the location of the 'third eye.' The next day when someone told Amma about this āśramite's '*darśan*,' she called him to her in order to check out his welt. When she saw it, she laughed uproariously and lovingly held him tight. Whenever Amma relates this story, she still laughs, but she always adds: "Such innocence should never be lost."

We may also laugh, thinking, 'My God! Amma taking the form of a *mosquito*? Give me a *break*! What a *rookie*!' But the scriptures tell us that all the five elements, which comprise the entirety of this physical world, are in fact divine in essence. A real Vedāntin should understand this truth and accept even a mosquito as divine in essence. (This doesn't mean he can't still chase it away.) So, a little of this type of innocence would not be such a bad thing.

HUMILITY

Eradicating the ego takes place on two levels. On the subtle level, it means to destroy the concept that one has a separate individuality. On the gross level, it means eradicating feelings of superiority[2]. In fact a strong gross ego is a sure sign one has a strong subtle ego.

[2] It should be noted that the feeling of inferiority is just as much a spiritual obstacle as the feeling of superiority.

Removal of the gross ego is the goal of spiritual life. This only comes with the assimilation of the knowledge that we are not the body, emotions and intellect, but consciousness, which in truth is all-pervading and eternal. In order to reach this understanding, we must first remove our gross ego, at least to some degree. This is why Amma stresses the importance of cultivating humility. Without humility, we can never bow down before the guru and accept that our concepts regarding reality are flawed. Where there is excess ego, one cannot even pick up the broom to engage in *guru seva.* As Amma says, "There is a huge tree dormant in the seed, but only if the seed is buried in the ground will the tree sprout. If the seed egotistically thinks, 'Why should I bow down to this dirty earth?' then its real nature cannot manifest and the seed may become food for a rat or squirrel. Likewise, only if we cultivate and develop humility is it possible to realize the Supreme Truth, which is our real nature."

Unfortunately some spiritual aspirants fall victim to pride. Completely identified with their minds and their intellectual understanding of spirituality, they develop subtle—and not so subtle—feelings of superiority. In Sādhana Pañcakam, Ādi Śaṅkarācārya specifically warns seekers against this pitfall, saying: *aharahargarvaḥ parityajyatām*—'May the arrogance of knowledge be constantly renounced by you.'

Humility is a natural expression of spiritual understanding. When we truly come to understand that the world and everyone in it are divine, how can we retain feelings of superiority? When we understand that without the five elements we cannot eat, drink or even breathe, how can we be anything but humble? When such pride comes, we should destroy it through reflection. We should think, "Any knowledge I possess has come from my guru alone. What claim can I lay to it? I cannot even claim responsibility for my mind and its ability to remember and think!"

Once there was a guru who had taken on two brothers as disciples. One morning the younger brother approached the guru and said, "I know you think my older brother is a more fit disciple than me. But what is so great about him? I can do anything he can do!"

The guru told the disciple to fetch his brother. Soon he returned with the older brother at his side. The guru said, "Each of you go out and wash the feet of 10 people who are inferior to you and we will see who returns first."

Both brothers bowed to their master and immediately set about their task. Barely one hour later, the younger brother returned. "I did it," he said. The guru just smiled compassionately.

It was after dusk when the older brother returned. He did not speak. He simply prostrated at his guru's feet. "Well?" asked the guru.

"I am sorry, Guruji," he said. "For the life of me, I could not find anyone inferior to me."

The guru looked at the younger brother and said, "It is his humility that makes him superior."

ALERTNESS

Amma says that a spiritual seeker should perform his every action with alertness. In this way, all of his actions become like a form of meditation. If we are truly serious about developing our mental focus, then we should live in a manner that transforms all of our so-called 'mundane' actions into vehicles of mental purification. In one upaniṣad, the spiritual path is even compared to "walking the edge of a blade." This is because one must not only hone his mind to a razor's sharpness but also then use that razor-sharp mind to constantly discriminate between reality and non-reality. Amma says if we don't develop alertness with regard to simple actions, we can never hope to do so with regards to our thoughts.

I remember a funny incident regarding a *brahmacāri* whose seva was to proofread an Āśram publication. When the publication came out, there was a horrible mistake in a quote of Amma's. What the quote was supposed to say was Amma's oft-heard statement:

"What we lack is not book knowledge but awareness." What the printed publication had Amma saying was: "What we lack is not awareness but book knowledge." What a sentence to botch! His proofreading itself—or lack of it—illustrated Amma's point. It's not that he didn't know Amma's teaching. He'd surely heard Amma saying this sentence many times before. But he lacked the awareness to even catch it when it was typed incorrectly. In fact, after the book was printed and the mistake was noticed, the brahmacāri had a nice time printing out little slips of paper with the correct sentence printed on them and pasting them over the incorrect sentences. Surely it was a lesson he will never forget.

COMPASSION

Amma says that compassion is love expressed as actions. True love is the feeling resulting from the experience of oneness. When someone we love suffers, we feel their pain as our own and do whatever we can to alleviate it. In fact, this is compassion's literal meaning, as the English word comes from the Latin *com* (together) + *pati* (to suffer). Whereas our love is limited—and that too reserved for a few people—a mahātma like Amma sees her oneness with the entire creation. As such, she naturally reaches out to serve the poor and suffering. Her actions are expansive due to the expansiveness of her mind. Her compassion has no borders because her concept of Self has no borders. Amma says that as we wish to expand our sense of Self, we should first try to open our heart and feel the pain of others. We should spend some time thinking about them and their sorrows, and, furthermore, do some selfless service to try to uplift them from their plight. A mahātma's vision is expansive and thus his actions follow suit. For us it can be like reverse engineering: Let our actions be expansive, and then slowly our minds will expand as well.

It goes without saying that Amma's entire life is a teaching in compassion. Compassionate actions in themselves breed compassion. At Amṛta Niketan, Amma's orphanage in Parippaḷḷi, Kollam District, Kerala, there is a beautiful example of this. The 500 orphans eat together three times a day. After every child is served, they chant the 15th chapter of the Bhagavad-Gīta and then offer two rice balls[3]. The first is for Amma; the second is offered to all the hungry children of the world. When the children close their eyes and pray for their fellow children, you see such sincerity on their faces. They are truly praying with all their hearts. Often you see tears rolling down their cheeks. Amma says we should all take time to reflect on the suffering of others. This will open our hearts and, in turn, manifest in our actions.

METHODS OF CULTIVATION

We can easily list dozens of good qualities we would like to have. But how to nurture those qualities to their full blossom within us?

The easiest method is *satsaṅg*—spending time with people who have those qualities. As already discussed in Chapter Two, the more we associate with *dharmic* [righteous] people, the more readily we imbibe dharmic behavior. Conversely, the more we associate with people with *adharmic* [unrighteous] qualities, the more likely we are to absorb adharmic behavior. Many Westerners who come to live in Amṛtapuri wind up developing slight Indian accents. Why? Association. Likewise, if we select good company, it can only benefit us, as we will absorb some of their good qualities. If we select poor company, it can easily bring us down. Even if our access to dharmic people is limited, we can always read about them in spiritual biographies. This is also satsaṅg.

Another thing we can do is to make a vow. If we really have a problem with patience, then we can solemnly make a vow that we will not lose our patience. After that we should try to be extra alert when getting into stressful, irritating or frustrating circumstances.

[3] The rice balls are eaten at the end of the meal as *prasād* [consecrated offering].

There is one āśramite who had a problem with anger. Not only did he often get angry, he would also often fly off the handle and lay into people with quite a poisonous tongue. After one such incident, Amma told him to start keeping a diary. Every night before he went to sleep he was to reflect on the day and write down all the times he had lost his temper. Amma also told him to write down every time he had made someone happy. In this way, she said it would be like a businessman looking over his books at night and reflecting on his earnings and losses. He would gradually gain awareness with regards to his actions. This was several years ago now. And, sure enough, today the āśramite is much kinder and more soft-spoken than he used to be—a real transformation. We can all adopt this diary technique. Just pick a quality and proceed. When we write each night, we can also do so as if writing directly to Amma. This will help deepen our bond with Amma.

When making a vow, it is best to be specific. Focus on one or two negative qualities to begin with. Otherwise we may feel overwhelmed. It is better to give ourselves specific targets. As we gain confidence, we can expand.

If we want to develop a particular value or good quality, we should also spend time reflecting on its benefits as well as the demerits of its negative counterpart. The clearer our mind becomes regarding the connection between the value and its positive benefits, the more likely we are to act accordingly. Similarly, the clearer we are regarding the demerit of a negative quality, the more readily we will abstain from it.

I remember once a woman asked Amma to help her overcome her addiction to coffee. Amma immediately asked her, "Why do you want to stop drinking coffee?" The woman had no clear answer. Amma's point seemed to be: Unless you know why you want to change, change will never take place. There are many reasons for giving up coffee—it causes nervousness, gives us headaches when we don't get it, induces insomnia, health problems, irritability, etc. If we want to overcome a negative habit, we should be clear regarding the reason why. If there is no clarity in thought, there can never be any clarity in action.

As spiritual seekers, we should spend time reflecting on how developing a desired quality will help lead us toward Self-realization. Conversely, we should reflect on how its negative counterpart will obstruct that goal. We need to develop a 'value for the value.' This will only happen if we spend time reflecting on the importance of the qualities. This is something we can do in the quietude of our meditation, but also any time of the day. We can even do it when the negative tendency we desire to overcome begins to arise. However if we only do it at such times, we may find that we do not have the strength to refrain from it. As with everything in life, we need practice.

Chapter Eight:

Sharpening the Mind

"Whatever form of meditation we do, whether we focus on the heart or between the eyebrows, the goal is the same: one-pointed concentration."

—Amma

WHEN MOST PEOPLE think of spirituality, the first thing that comes to their mind is meditation. Unfortunately meditation is one of the most misunderstood aspects of spiritual life. What exactly is meditation? What is its purpose? Is it an end or a means? How does it work? Ostensibly it is such a mysterious process. Fortunately, in Amma we have a living master who can provide us with proper tailor-made guidance based on her own experience.

In essence there are two types of meditation—meditation on God with form and meditation on the *ātma*—the very consciousness that serves as the center of our being. These are called *saguṇa* meditation and *nirguṇa* meditation, respectively[1]. Amma's Mā-Om Meditation, the Integrated Amrita Meditation Technique® (IAM Technique®), mental *mantra japa* and *mānasa pūja* [mental worship] are all various types of saguṇa meditation. Saguṇa indicates that the object of our meditation has concrete qualities. In such meditations, there is a clear difference between our self—the meditator—and the object of our meditation. For example, in Mā-Om Meditation—the short meditation Amma leads everyone through during her programs—we meditate on the

[1] Saguṇa means 'with qualities'; nirguṇa means 'without qualities.'

ingoing and outgoing breath coupled with the syllables *mā* and *om*, respectively. In IAM Technique®, we are given an evolving series of locations within the physical body upon which to concentrate. When we do japa or *arcana*, we are focusing on one or multiple mantras. When we engage in mānasa pūja, we are mentally trying to picture and worship the form of our beloved deity.

Just as *karma yoga* is aimed at refining the mind through the removal of our likes and dislikes, saguṇa meditation also has its intended purpose. Primarily this lies in improving our power of one-pointed concentration. "Whichever point of the body we meditate upon, the goal is one-pointed concentration," Amma says. In fact, this is the aim of the majority of mental spiritual practices.

Along these lines there is a story that appears in the Bible[2]. When Jesus was travelling throughout Galilee, he came to a place where there was a man who was said to be possessed by demonic forces. He lived among the tombs, ranting and raving and generally scaring everyone who lived around there half to death. After some time he approached Jesus, and Jesus asked him what his name was. And the man said, "Call me 'Legion,' for we are many." What the Bible says he meant by this was that he wasn't possessed by merely one demon but by a multitude of demons. Regardless, Jesus blessed the man, and the legion of demons was cast out. Some people see a symbolic significance to this exorcism. The legion of demons represents a nonintegrated mind. Such a mind contains a multitude of conflicting impulses and ideas. It has no power of focus, nor can it ever be relaxed. Legion's example is extreme, but if we introspect we will see that most of us are 'possessed' in this way to some extent. Meeting with Jesus means coming into contact with a *mahātma*, whose teachings help us gain mental control, focus and, ultimately, peace.

---

[2] Mark, 5.1-20 and Luke 8.26-39

If one wants to be successful in any field, worldly or spiritual, the ability to concentrate is essential. A financial analyst must be able to focus on the stock-market reports; a baseball player or cricket batsman must be able to focus on the ball; a computer programmer must be able to focus on the code. Similarly a disciple must be able to focus on the teachings of his guru throughout his day-to-day life. Everything requires concentration.

The scriptures repeatedly tell us that we are not the mind. Rather, the mind is a tool for us to use in order to transact with the world around us. In this way, it is much like a computer. Any computer-savvy person knows that a computer needs regular maintenance. We have to defragment hard drives, clean up unwanted files, update the system software, maybe even increase the RAM and memory, etc. Furthermore we have to regularly update the anti-virus software. Just as such practices keep our computers free from breakdown, regular meditation keeps the mental computer happy and healthy.

Meditation can also be compared to physical exercise. We all know that if we want to keep the body healthy, we have to keep up a basic regimen of exercise. This is something that everyone needs. But as spiritual seekers, we are different. We are not merely interested in maintaining basic mental health; we want to create a mind capable of realizing the ultimate truth—freeing us to revel in the bliss of the Self.

There is a portion in the Śrīmad Bhāgavatam, which was written several thousand years ago, wherein Sage Śuka is talking about the oncoming age and how materialistic it will be. In this passage, he gives a long list of predictions. When we look at these, it is shocking to see how many have already come true—especially when we consider the piety of the times in which the Bhāgavatam was written. One of the things Śuka says about our age is:

snānam-eva prasādhanam |

"Mere bathing makes one ready."

[Śrīmad Bhāgavatam, 12.2.5]

The meaning is that, in today's age, very few people care about internal purity—only external. No one places importance on purifying and cleaning up the mind, only the body.

Amma says that our minds should become like the remote control to a television, resting firmly in the palm of our hand. That means total mental control—the ability to mentally respond in perfect accordance with any given situation. If we want to think about something, we should be able to do so with focus—whether it be for five minutes or five hours. If we want to recall some past event, we should be able to do so. And perhaps most importantly, we should immediately be able to—with the click of a button—turn the thing off and relax! This type of mental refinement is the purpose of saguṇa meditation. So the path is clear: from the relative insanity of 'Legion' to the remote-control mind.

Saguṇa meditation does not directly bring about Self-realization. Self-realization is just that—a *realization*, a permanent shift in understanding. It is the firm knowledge that we are not the body, emotions or intellect but pure blissful, eternal consciousness. This is something that Amma tells us every day. She even begins every public talk by saying, "Amma bows down to everyone whose nature is divine love and the Self." Many of us have heard or read such statements regarding our divinity thousands of times by now, yet we still remain the same grumpy, irritable, frustrated people. If this knowledge really liberates, why are we still suffering mentally? Amma herself gives us the answer. She says, "Children, what you lack is not knowledge, but awareness." What does Amma mean by awareness? She means the ability to never—not even in the most stressful, action-packed, potentially fatal of circumstances—forget the truth of who we are. As is said in the Bhagavad-Gīta:

naiva kiṁcit-karomīti yukto manyeta tattvavit |
paśyañ-śṛṇvan-spṛśaṇ-jighrannaśnan-gacchan-svapañśvasan ||
pralapan-visṛjan-ghṛṇannunmiṣan-nimiṣannapi |
indriyāṇīndriyārtheṣu vartanta iti dhārayan ||

"Even while seeing, hearing, touching, smelling, eating, going, sleeping, breathing, speaking, emptying, holding, opening and closing the eyes, the sage remains centered in the Self, knowing, 'The senses are moving among the sense objects, yet I do nothing at all.'"

[Bhagavad-Gīta, 5.8-9]

This is the awareness that Amma is telling us we need to cultivate. Most of us can intellectually understand Vedānta, but when the body experiences pain, we forget the truth "I am not the body." Most of us can intellectually understand how we are not the emotions, but when someone wrongs us, we forget this truth and lose our temper. Most of us can even understand that the center of who we are is beyond the intellectual ideas popping in and out of our head, but how many of us can maintain this awareness throughout the day? In essence, the problem is a deficiency in our power of awareness—our inability to remain focused on this teaching as we conduct our lives.

It is through our various mental spiritual practices that we hone our power of concentration. When it is properly developed we can then use that power to maintain awareness regarding our true nature throughout our daily lives. In his commentary on Chāndogya Upaniṣad, Ādi Śaṅkarācārya defines saguṇa meditation as "establishing a continuous flow of similar modifications of the mind [i.e. thoughts] in relation to some object as presented by the scriptures and uninterrupted by any foreign idea." Śaṅkara then reveals that Self-realization is also continuance of a mere mental modification—the knowledge that one's true nature is blissful, eternal consciousness. He says that the only difference between this mental modification and other modifications is that when we constantly abide in thoughts of our true nature, it demolishes all sense of division between us, the world, the people around us, and God. With the demolition of these divisions comes the demolition of all the afflictions springing from them, such as anger, depression, loneliness, jealousy and frustration.

This concept of honing the mind through saguṇa meditation and then using that refined mind to focus on the scriptural teachings is explained in Muṇḍaka Upaniṣad[3] through a metaphor involving a bow, arrow and target. In essence, the upaniṣad advises us to sharpen the arrow of the mind through saguṇa meditation and then, using the mighty bow of spiritual wisdom that is the upaniṣads, make it merge in the target—imperishable, all-pervading, blissful consciousness.

The Gīta also clearly defines the role of saguṇa meditation along the same lines:

> tatraikāgraṁ manaḥ kṛtvā yata-cittendriya-kriyaḥ |
> upaviśyāsane yuñjyād-yogam-ātma-viśuddhaye ||
>
> *"Sitting there on his seat, making the mind one-pointed and restraining the thinking faculty and the senses, he should practice yoga for self-purification."*
>
> [Bhagavad-Gīta, 6.12]

Saguṇa meditation is a stepping stone—the 'sharpening of the arrow.' Just like karma yoga, it purifies our mental equipment. Even though karma yoga and saguṇa meditation do not directly bring about Self-realization, one would have to be foolish to say they are not important. They are *essential.* Without them, we will

[3] Muṇḍaka Upaniṣad, 2.2.3-4

never be able to attain the goal we are seeking. Our favorite part of *pūja* [worship] may be eating the *prasād* [consecrated offering], but unless we go through all the preceding steps—the invocation, the offerings, the prayers, the *ārati*, etc.—the prasād in fact is not prasād at all, but just food. Similarly, the fruit of knowledge will only come if we've done the essential preceding steps. Amma often compares these steps to cleaning the vessel (i.e. the mind) before adding the milk (wisdom). "If we pour milk into a dirty vessel, the milk will spoil," Amma says. "We have to clean the vessel before transferring milk into it. Those who desire to be spiritually uplifted should first try to purify themselves. To purify the mind is to eliminate negative and unnecessary thoughts and to reduce selfishness and desires."

Some people say they are not interested in performing saguṇa meditation. They say that they will refine their power of concentration using thoughts regarding their true nature. However Śaṅkara says that, at least in the beginning of spiritual life, it is better to improve our power of concentration through these saguṇa meditations. This is because contemplation on something without name or form is extremely subtle and, therefore, all the more difficult. Unless the mind is properly refined, attempts at contemplation on the formless reality often result only in sleep or stupor. On the other hand, saguṇa meditations—concentrating on a form or name of God, on the breath or locations in the body, etc.—are relatively easy. Thus until our power of concentration is perfected, we can use these types of meditation to improve it. As we will see in Chapter Nine, when one is ready, nirguṇa meditation [meditation on the formless Self] is supposed to be done *constantly*—even while walking, talking, eating, sitting, etc. With this in mind, it is very relevant that Amma instructs us to not only set aside some time for formal mantra japa (i.e. seated with eyes closed), but also to try to perform it "with every breath." In fact, this is preparing our mind for that constant nirguṇa meditation, which comes as the ultimate spiritual practice.

Śaṅkara also says that as our minds become more and more refined through saguṇa meditations they can come to provide us with "a glimpse of the reality of the Self." Such glimpses will fill us with inspiration to persevere in our practices with more and more intensity and enthusiasm.

THE YOGA SŪTRAS

Perhaps the foremost authority on saguṇa meditation was Sage Patañjali. It was Patañjali who authored the Yoga Sūtras, outlining a step-by-step process for success in meditation. It is from these sūtras [aphorisms] that the oft-heard phrase '*aṣṭāṅga yoga*' [the yoga of eight steps] comes. According to Patañjali, meditation should be approached in eight consecutive steps: *yama, niyama, āsana, prāṇāyāma, pratyāhāra, dhāraṇa, dhyāna* and then *samādhi.* Respectively, these translate as don'ts, do's, posture, breath-control, withdrawal of senses, mental focus, continued mental focus and absorption.

YAMA

According to Patañjali, if we hope to establish a successful meditation practice, we should first make sure we are following the five yamas and five niyamas—specific don'ts and do's. The yamas—the don'ts—are *ahimsa, satya, asteya, brahmacarya* and *aparigraha.*

Ahimsa means 'non-violence.' In order to be successful in meditation, we should avoid violence. This is one of the most important rules for all human beings to follow. With few exceptions, we should always avoid harming anyone. This is important not only for the harmonious growth of society but also for our inner growth. The ultimate truth proclaimed by the sages is that we are all one in essence. If we wish to realize this truth, we should begin treating each other as one. Would anyone in his right mind ever intentionally harm himself? And if this was not reason enough to abstain from violence, there is always the fact that our violent actions will come back to us as per the dictates of the law of karma.

When attempting to live a life of non-violence, we should approach it on three levels—physical violence, verbal violence and mental violence. If someone cuts us off in traffic and we then begin trying to ram him off the road, then that is physical violence. Most of us are probably able to refrain from such activity. (However, how many of us perhaps punch the steering wheel after such an incident? Or even offer some 'loving' gestures?) Verbal violence would be shouting out the window certain choice words. Mental violence is the most subtle form of violence and therefore the most difficult to overcome. It is any thought of ill will—imagining either physical or verbal violence upon him. We often tolerate our mental *himsa* [violence] because we think it has no negative effect, but if we allow it to go unchecked, eventually it will manifest on the verbal or physical level. As Amma said in her address at the Millennium World Peace Summit in the United Nations General Assembly in New York in 2000, "Simply transferring the world's nuclear weapons to a museum will not in itself bring about world peace. The nuclear weapons of the mind must first be eliminated."

The second yama is satyam—telling the truth, or not lying. Definitely, we should only speak truth. However, before speaking truth, we should consider who will be helped and who will be harmed if we speak it. If more people will be benefited than harmed, we can speak. If more people will be harmed, better keep quiet. As Amma says, "Just because someone looks like a monkey, there is no need to go up to him and tell him so." If no one will be helped, then it is probably not worth saying at all; we should just hold our tongue. There is no need to add to the noise pollution plaguing the planet. Truth is human nature. When we lie, we are moving against our true nature. As such, it is as if we are introducing an impurity into our system.

The third yama is asteya—non-stealing. There is a beautiful saying that the only sin is stealing. When we kill, we steal someone's right to life. When we lie, we steal someone's right to truth. When we cheat, we steal someone's right to fairness. Stealing takes place whenever we acquire anything through illegitimate means. Stealing is a universal taboo. Even the thief knows it is wrong, otherwise he would not mind when one of his fellow thieves happens to rip him off.

The next yama is brahmacārya. Brahmacārya is typically taken as celibacy, but total celibacy is not required of all sections of society. So, here, we can define brahmacārya as avoidance of any sexual behavior inappropriate for our place in society. This will vary from culture to culture. Certainly *brahmacāris* [disciple students] and *sannyāsis* [monks] are prohibited from any such activity. There is nothing wrong in married couples showing physical affection for one another, but they are supposed to reserve such affection for their spouse alone. And it should be remembered that Amma says that one should enter marriage in order to overcome desire, not to become further mired in it.

The final yama is aparigraha—non-hoarding. Possessing things is fine, but, again, we should not possess beyond certain limits. In general, Amma tells us to try to get by with the minimum, specifically with regard to luxuries. Frequently Amma asks women to try to reduce the number of outfits they purchase each year and men to give up cigarettes and alcohol. The money saved, Amma suggests, can be donated to charity.

These five yamas are basic human values and in fact should be followed by one and all, not just by meditators. But from the perspective of successful meditation, they have specific importance. If we violate any of the first four yamas—non-violence, truthfulness, non-stealing, fidelity—it will typically make a deep impression in our mind, which will then come back to the surface during our attempts at meditation, becoming an obstacle to attaining one-pointed focus. This can either be the prick of a guilty conscience or simply the resurgence of the memory. The final yama, aparigraha, disturbs the mind because when we hoard things we are in fact allowing our desires to get out of control. During our attempts at meditation this will manifest either as a fear of losing what we have hoarded or thoughts of hoarding more.

NIYAMA

Next we have the five niyamas—the *do's* for practitioners of meditation. The first is *śaucam*—cleanliness. The scriptures say that we should keep our body, clothes and physical surroundings clean. Not only is uncleanliness unhealthy for us and for others, but it also disturbs our mind. When our work area is untidy, we will find that we become easily distracted as well. Conversely, the more tidy it is, the more naturally focused our mind. For most people the mind cannot be organized unless our environment is first. So, before we sit for meditation, we should make sure that our surroundings are clean.

The second niyama is *santoṣam*—contentment. Amma says that contentment is a mental attitude. We cannot always make the external world conform to our likes and dislikes, but the internal world should be under our control. If one is seeking success in meditation, it is vital that he makes the resolve to remain joyful in life come what may. That is not to say we shouldn't strive for success or change. We should strive to excel in our professions and chosen fields of actions, however we should not connect success and failure in those fields with our mental peace. Try hard, but come success or failure, be content. Santoṣam goes hand-in-hand with the yama aparigraha, in that, if we learn to be content with the minimum in terms of luxuries, we will be able to use the rest of our resources for the benefit of society. Cultivating contentment is important because if we truly analyze the human mind, we will see (as discussed in Chapter Five) that no one can ever gain contentment through possessions. No matter how much one gets, he will always want more. As soon as we get a raise at work, we start thinking about the next one. The congressman wants to become a senator, the senator wants to become president, and the president wants to rule the world. When we come to understand this truth, we will begin to try to cultivate a contentment that is not based on money or possessions. A mind that is not at least relatively content will never be able to focus in meditation.

The third niama is *tapas*—austerity. It is only through austerities that we are able to keep our mind and sense organs in control. When we set no limits on ourselves, we become like a child let loose in a candy store. The result is a mess and a sick child. In the same way when man doesn't control himself, he only winds up harming society and himself. There is a nice saying in India: "Let the goats roam free and they will turn the yard into a mess; tie them to a post and they will clean the area nicely." Only through abstention do we gain true mental strength. This is the significance of all the various vows people take in religious life. Amma recommends selecting one day a week to spend in fasting and silence. When we know we can go without something, it no longer has any control over us. During meditation we want to be 100 percent focused on a single mental object. Unless we have gained a relative amount of control over our mind and sense organs, through refusing to always give in to their wants, we will never be able to focus during actual meditation.

The fourth niyama is *svādhyāya*. Literally svādhyāya means 'self study.' Studying the scriptures and words of our guru is not an extrovert activity. The guru and scriptures are the mirror with which we look inside and see who we really are. Amma says that a serious seeker should spend some time studying the scriptures and guru's teachings every day. In fact this is the first instruction in Ādi Śaṅkarācārya's Sādhana Pañcakam: *vedo nityam adhīyatām*—"May you study the scriptures daily." Only through their study will we come to know the ultimate goal of life and how to reach it. Furthermore we can neither meditate nor understand meditation's place in the spiritual path unless we first learn these things from a proper source—be it Amma or the traditional scriptures.

The final observance is *īśvara praṇidhānam*—surrender to God. This means to do all actions as worship of the Lord. In essence this indicates the karma-yoga attitude, as in karma yoga we surrender our actions to the Lord and accept whatever results come as *prasād.* As said in Chapter Five, it is through applying the karma-yoga attitude that we overcome our likes and dislikes. Unless we gain control over these, we will never have a mind peaceful enough to sit in focused meditation.

ĀSANA

The next step in Patañjali's system is āsana. Āsana means 'posture' or 'seat.' Before beginning our meditation, we should make sure that we are able to sit steadily in a proper posture. Just as Kṛṣṇa advises Arjuna in the sixth chapter of the Gīta, Amma always advises us to sit straight and still, with our spine, neck and head aligned. Amma recommends that the chin be slightly raised as well. We can either rest our hands folded in our lap or rest them on our thighs with our palms turned upward. Sitting in this posture takes the weight of the chest off the lungs, allowing our breath to be light and easy throughout our meditation. The position of the hands and the straightness of the spine are also conducive to the proper upward flow of *prāṇa* [energy], which is conducive to meditation. One can sit in any comfortable position—with legs simply crossed or in half-lotus or in *padmāsana* [full-lotus] if possible. There should be no strain. So don't force yourself into any position you can't easily get out of. There is no use sitting in a posture that is only going to cause you to meditate on discomfort. It is also certainly fine to sit in a chair if necessary, but one should avoid leaning against the back of the chair, as this easily leads to sleep. In the Gīta, Kṛṣṇa says that the cushion or mat we sit upon should be neither too soft nor too hard. Sitting directly upon the floor or earth, without some sort of mat or rug, is also not recommended. Masters in meditation say that, just as an electrical circuit loses power when grounded, so too the energy in the body is weakened when the body comes in direct contact with the ground.

Āsana can also refer to *haṭha-yoga* āsanas—what one typically thinks of when they hear the word 'yoga.' A regular haṭha-yoga practice is an excellent way to maintain health and vitality. But we should make sure that we are taught by a true haṭha-yoga master, as these stretches are quite subtle and if done incorrectly can have adverse ramifications. We should also note that haṭha yoga in the context of Patañjali's aṣṭāṅga system is not an end in itself. Rather it is to be performed as a *preparation* for seated meditation—loosening up the body so that it can sit properly for our chosen duration of meditation, stimulating conducive flow of prāṇa and slowly turning the mind inward. This is the aim of all the āsanas given in Amma's IAM Technique®.

PRĀṆĀYĀMA

After āsana, the next step is prāṇāyāma, which means 'breath-control.' Like haṭha yoga, prāṇāyāma has extremely subtle effects and can be harmful if not done properly under direct observance of an experienced master. Today, many individuals and institutions are teaching very subtle prāṇāyāma techniques to anyone willing to pay the fees. Amma feels this is very dangerous and often warns people about this problem. Simple prāṇāyāma can be practiced by almost everyone[4], but involved, extended prāṇāyāma is traditionally prescribed on a one-on-one basis according to one's physical and vital capacity and ability of control. Amma warns us to be particularly careful to avoid forcefully holding the

[4] People with heart conditions, asthma, high-blood pressure, or women who are pregnant should consult their physicians.

breath either after inhalation or after exhalation. Amma says, "In the old days when the guru was going to initiate someone into prāṇāyāma, he would make him go get a fiber from the shell of a brown coconut husk or perhaps a blade of grass or a thread. The guru would then hold this under the disciple's nose and observe the various aspects of his breath—such as strength, duration, length and nature of the flow from each nostril—upon it. Only after this would he prescribe the requisite style, duration and number of repetitions."

In the meditation techniques taught by Amma, we find that Amma does not advise involved prāṇāyāma. Other than an extremely short, forceful prāṇāyāma toward the beginning of IAM Technique®, Amma mainly advises *prāṇa vīkṣaṇa*—breathing normally with awareness. In fact, this is a core part of the Mā-Om Technique. The breaths should be even and smooth. In Mā-Om, Amma has us couple our inhalations with the mental chanting of the *bījākṣara* [seed syllable] *mā* and our exhalations with the mental chanting of *om*. This type of prāṇāyāma is known as *sagarbha* prāṇāyāma—literally, prāṇāyāma 'impregnated' with mantra. When we consider how the meditation techniques taught by Amma came to her intuitively, it is amazing to see how perfectly they align with practices found in the various traditional scriptures. Such things are really a testament to the statement that a sadguru is a living scripture.

In Patañjali's system, prāṇāyāma—just like āsana—is not an end in itself, but a step aimed at slowly drawing the mind more and more inward. Haṭha yoga is done focusing the mind on the external body. In prāṇāyāma, the locus of our focus becomes subtler—the very life-force *inside* the body. In this way we see Patañjali is systematically moving us gradually, step by step, inward, thus increasing the practice's subtlety and, consequently, its impact.

PRATYĀHĀRA

The next step is pratyāhāra—withdrawal of the senses. This is just common sense—we cannot begin to focus on something in the mind if we are still actively contacting the outside world through the eyes, ears, nose, tongue and skin. The eyes we can close. And most likely we can avoid eating anything during our practice. However if we are disturbed through the senses of touch, smell or hearing, it will be difficult for us to meditate. This is why the scriptures instruct us to meditate in at least relative solitude or in the early morning when the rest of the world is sleeping. The place should also be clean. Dirty places often have foul smells, perhaps even mosquitoes—a persistent foe of the meditator. In this way we can curb the naturally extroverted nature of the sense organs, allowing the mind to focus on our chosen object of meditation.

However Amma says we need to develop the ability to meditate in any environment. When I first joined the āśram, the villagers used to leave heaps of coconut husks in the backwaters. The salty water helps decompose the husks, making them easier to shred and then weave into coconut-fiber rope. Well, let me tell you, few things stink worse than a heap of rotting coconut husks! And the sound of the ladies pounding the husks was still further assault upon the senses. Yet Amma would have us sit right near there and meditate for a couple of hours at a stretch. In Amma's opinion, one should not postpone his meditation for lack of quietude or 'suitable location.' When our scheduled meditation time comes, we should be able to withdraw our mind and focus, regardless of where we may be. By asking us to meditate near the rotting husks, Amma was helping us to develop that capacity.

DHĀRAṆA

The next step is dhāraṇa—mental focus. Here, the idea is to simply apply the unencumbered mind to the chosen field. It can be the mental image of a god, goddess or guru. It can be our breath or mantra. It could be physical locations in our body. The Vedas enumerate hundreds of such objects for our meditation[5]. It can be any object, but the scriptures tell us that we should make a mental note of connecting that object with the divine. This is why, in Amma's Mā-Om Meditation, Amma always takes the time to state that the sound *om* is a symbol for divine light (i.e. consciousness) and that the sound *mā* represents divine love. It's not that thereafter we think about consciousness or divine love; we simply focus our minds on the breath coupled with the sound *mā* and *om*. But we have made the *saṅkalpa* [resolve] of what they represent.

DHYĀNA

Dhāraṇa is simply one thought. The next step, dhyāna, is actually continuance in that thought. As Śaṅkara says: "Establishing a continuous flow of similar modifications of the mind [i.e. thoughts] in relation to some object as presented by the scriptures and uninterrupted by any foreign idea." At the dhyāna stage, the mind is maintaining a single thought, but it is maintained only due to our effort. It is a struggle.

I am sure we have all had similar experiences to the following: We are sitting in meditation, trying to mentally focus on, for example, Devi's form. We concentrate on her crown, her hair, then her *sāri*... Seeing the sāri in our mind we think, *Oh, Devi's sāri is so beautiful. A beautiful deep blue... Blue like the sea...* And then our sneaky mind comes in: *Remember last summer when I took a sea cruise to Venezuela...* And then we start thinking of a restaurant we ate in there... And then some interesting people we met there... *That fellow at the restaurant had a really nice watch... Oh, I really need to get a new watch... Maybe I should go to the mall tomorrow... The last time I went to the mall, I got into a fight*

[5] Predominantly in the *araṅyaka* sections.

with my sister, Devika... Oops! We suddenly remember we were supposed to be meditating on Devi.

This is how the mind is—a flow of thoughts. Normally the flow is totally wild—a mere stream of thoughts based upon mental associations and *vāsanas* [mental tendencies]. Through practice we can develop the ability to channel this flow of thoughts toward one object. This is like providing rails for the train; they ensure we stay on course and arrive at our intended destination. As our power of awareness increases, so too does our ability to catch the mind when it veers off course. When we can consistently restrict our focus to our chosen mental field, it is referred to as dhyāna.

SAMĀDHI

The culmination of saguṇa meditation is samādhi—complete effortless absorption in our chosen thought. Here the mind flows forth unimpeded, the traditional imagery being that of the unflickering flame of an oil lamp burning inside a glass case. Until this stage of meditation, there are always two—the meditator and the object of meditation. But in samādhi, the meditator forgets himself completely and the object of meditation becomes his sole existing reality. This is the culmination of saguṇa meditation. Even in our daily life, at moments, while watching television or a movie, we become so absorbed in what is happening that we forget ourselves completely. Before we know it, two hours have passed. Obviously the difference between watching TV and meditation is that it is the natural lower tendency of the mind and sense organs to go outward, and in meditation we are training them to go inward. That said, we have all experienced moments in which we become lost in thought—perhaps, in an intellectual idea or a daydream—but as long as our concentration is unwilled, it will never bring about the mental refinement we are seeking through saguṇa meditation.

It is important to note that samādhi in meditation should not be confused with Self-realization. Self-realization is a shift in our understanding, wherein we come to comprehend our true nature, the nature of the world around us and the nature of God as all being blissful, eternal consciousness in essence. It is called an advaitic—non-dual—experience because we see once and for all that the only thing that exists within and without is consciousness. This understanding is permanent and remains with us whether we are sitting with eyes closed in meditation or eating or sleeping or walking or talking. In Patañjali's samādhi, one's experience of bliss is due to the mind's one-pointed concentration. Focused on one point, the mind becomes so still that the bliss of the Self shines through the mental equipment that normally obscures it. As such, we get, as Śaṅkara says, "a glimpse of the reality of the Self." However, when one stops meditating and opens his eyes, the dualistic world returns, the glimpse ends and we continue to be the same person, with all our negativities. This is why it is said that permanent bliss can only come from knowledge. The source of this misconception—regarding samādhi in meditation being the same as Self-realization—is that Self-realization is also at times referred to as 'samādhi.' However, technically, Self-realization is called *sahaja samādhi*—a 'natural samādhi' born out of the understanding that all is one.

Actually it is a rather beautiful and fascinating concept. In meditative samādhi we limit the mind to one thought and experience bliss as a result. In sahaja samādhi we understand that everything we see and think of is really of one essence and thus experience bliss. In the former we reduce plurality to one through discipline, in the latter we reduce it to one through understanding. Meditative samādhi is transitory; it ends upon the meditation's conclusion. Samādhi founded on understanding, however, once attained, never ends.

Amma often says that most people attain only a minute or two of real concentration during an hour-long meditation session. She says that real meditation is not simply sitting with eyes closed, but "a state of unbroken concentration like an endless stream"—i.e.

Patañjali's samādhi. But, still, that is alright, Amma says. Our power of concentration will grow with time and practice. Amma often explains this by saying, "Suppose we put some water on the stove to make tea. If someone asks what we are doing, we would say that we are making tea. Actually, the water is only getting heated up; it is only the beginning. We have not yet added the tea leaves, milk or sugar. Even then, we will say that we are making tea. Likewise, we say that we are meditating, but it is only the beginning. We have not yet reached the state of real meditation."

OTHER SPIRITUAL PRACTICES

Increasing our power of focus is the goal of the majority of spiritual practices. Meditation is a purely mental activity; concentration on the object of meditation must be attained with the mind alone. However, with other practices we rely on various sense organs for support.

For example, Amma widely recommends the daily chanting of the Lalita Sahasranāma—The Thousands Names of the Divine Mother. In this practice, we not only *think* of the mantras, but we also chant them aloud, thus involving both the *karmendriya* [organ of action] of the tongue and the *jñānendriya* [organ of knowledge] of the ear. We may also read the mantras, thus drawing upon the support of the organ of the eyes as well. Some people go through the physical motion of pretending to offer flower petals with each name they chant—drawing upon the support of the action-organ of the hands as well. The more sense organs we involve, the easier it will be to get one-pointed concentration. The singing of *bhajans* works on the same principle. This is why many people who have difficulty attaining one-pointed concentration in meditation prefer chanting mantras or singing bhajans. The general rule is this: The more senses involved, the easier it will be to concentrate. Conversely, the fewer senses we use, the more powerful the practice.

To understand this, it is helpful to think of someone engaged in physical exercise. The more individual muscles he uses to lift a weight, the easier it will be to do so. At the same time, the fewer muscles he engages to lift that same weight, the more of a workout the muscles he does use will receive. In spiritual practices we are not really interested in refining the power of our hearing or eyesight, etc. We want to strengthen the mind. So, the fewer sense organs we draw upon, the more of a workout the mind will get. This is why Ramaṇa Maharṣi wrote in his treatise Upadeśa Sāram:

uttama stavāducca mandataḥ |
cittajaṁ japa-dhyānam-uttamam ||

"Loud repetition is better than praise. Better still is its faint muttering. But the best is mental repetition; it is verily meditation." [Upadeśa Sāram, 6]

And this is the same advice Amma gives us when we take mantra *dīkṣa* [initiation] from her. She says, "In the beginning chant the mantra so that only you can hear the sound. Once you are able to do it like that with one-pointed focus, then chant it only by moving the lips, like a fish. After you become firmly established in that, make it a habit to chant it only mentally." We can take this in two ways. 'Beginning' can mean the initial period following our initiation into the mantra. Or it can mean the beginning of our daily mantra-japa practice. So, in general, as we progress in the macrocosm of our life, we should try to make our spiritual practices more refined and subtle. At the same time, this may be reflected in the microcosm of our daily practice.

Just as chanting a mantra mentally is more powerful than chanting it orally, similarly, it is said that chanting one mantra over and over again is more powerful than chanting a string of mantras. This is because the nature of the mind is a flow. It is always looking for something new. Once it has sucked the juice out of one thing, it wants to go on to something new. The more we limit the mind, the less we are allowing it to adhere to this extrovert nature. Through all these practices it is as if we are applying mental brakes, wrestling the mind into a course of *our* choosing. Previously we have not been in control; it has been, as Amma says, "a case of the tail wagging the dog." When we apply the brakes, heat will result. The heat is a sign that the mind is being purified. It is not a coincidence that the Sanskrit word for 'heat' and the word for 'austerity' are one and the same—tapas. This doesn't mean everyone who likes to chant aloud should stop doing so. We have to introspect, honestly evaluate our level and then move forward, trying to intensify our practices over time.

That said, Amma says there is a special benefit to chanting the Lalita Sahasranāma aloud. She says that when it is done so with the proper rhythm and pace, it almost is like a form of prāṇāyāma, effortlessly regulating the breath and, thereby, relaxing and purifying the body and mind.

OBSTACLES IN MEDITATION

Meditation is one of the subtlest spiritual practices. For some it is a source of great bliss, for others a source of great frustration. The majority fall somewhere between these two extremes. In his commentary on Māṇḍūkya Upaniṣad, the grand-guru of Ādi Śaṅkarācārya, Śrī Gauḍapādācārya, mentions four specific obstacles to meditation as well as remedies. They are *laya, vikṣepa, kaṣāya* and *rasāsvada.*

Laya means sleep. Most of us are all too familiar with this problem, particularly when we first begin practicing meditation. It is only natural. Our entire life we have only associated closing our eyes and relaxing with sleeping. Now we suddenly want to close the eyes and yet remain alert. Thus, we often find ourselves snoring away. To overcome this obstacle, we have to look to the cause of sleep.

Sleep in meditation typically comes from either insufficient sleep at night, too much food, excessive physical exertion or health problems, like low blood pressure, etc. With regard to this problem, Amma most often tells people to stand up and move around for some time. "If you feel sleepy, get up and walk while chanting your mantra; then the *tamas* [lethargy] will go away. In the initial stages of meditation, all your tamasic qualities will surface. If you are vigilant, they will vanish in due course. When you feel sleepy, chant the mantra using a *japa māla* [necklace of prayer beads]." If our object of meditation is an image, Amma recommends opening our eyes and focusing them upon the external image. Once the sleepiness passes, we can close our eyes and resume with the inner visualization.

I remember in the early days of the āśram, Amma would sit with us during our meditations and keep a bag of pebbles at her side. If someone began falling asleep, Amma would toss one at him—always with excellent aim. Sometimes we still see this at Amma's programs. Since *darśan* typically goes to three or four in the morning, many people meditating around Amma will begin drifting off. Amma has her own unique way of waking them—throwing some piece of candy at them as prasād.

The second obstacle is vikṣepa [agitation]. Here the mind is not sleepy. It is just the opposite; we cannot focus due to mental agitation. The root cause of mental agitation occurs due to desire. As discussed earlier, desire comes due to confusion regarding the true source of happiness—i.e. the misconception that its source is sense objects rather than the Self. In order to remove this problem during meditation, Gauḍapāda recommends that we reflect on the impermanence of the objects distracting our thoughts and how they will only lead to sorrow in the end. Amma's advice is the same: "When unwanted thoughts arise during meditation, we should think, 'O mind, is there any benefit in cherishing these thoughts? Do these have any value?' By thinking like this, you should reject unnecessary thoughts. Complete dispassion must come. Detachment should arise. The conviction that the sense objects are equal to poison should become firmly rooted in the mind."

Next comes kaṣāya. In kaṣāya the mind is neither sleepy, nor distracted by thoughts, yet still one is not attaining deep meditative absorption because the desires still remain in the subconscious mind. Here, the only remedy is to witness the mind in this state and then when the latent desires surface in the conscious mind remove them through discriminative thinking.

The final obstacle Gauḍapāda mentions is rasāsvada, which literally means 'tasting (*asvadana*) the bliss (*rasa*).' When the mind becomes absorbed in one's chosen object of meditation, peace and bliss will be experienced. When this happens we should not allow ourselves to become distracted by its intoxicating effect. We should retain our focus on our chosen object of meditation. We always have to remember the intention behind our meditation practice: to sharpen the mind. In fact, the bliss we experience at such times is really a reflection of the bliss of the Self as experienced in the mirror of the mind. It will come and it will go depending on our mental state. 'Tasting' the bliss is not our goal. Ultimately we have to go beyond this and realize our identity as the ātma, the true source of all blissful experiences. As will be explained in detail in Chapter Nine, this is not an experience, but a shift in understanding. Saguṇa meditation prepares our mind for this shift, but does not actually create this shift in itself. This has to come through knowledge.

In fact, Amma says that any action if done with the proper resolve and attitude can become a spiritual practice as long as it is done with awareness. Walking can be performed as a spiritual practice, talking can be performed as a spiritual practice, so too eating or doing household chores. Definitely, if performed with concentration and awareness of the goal, anything can help refine our mind.

Amma's entire life is a demonstration of this principle. Everything she does is done with such care and focus. To the casual eye, it may not look so because Amma is so natural in her actions. But if we really look, we will see that everything Amma does—her casual glances, spontaneous smiles, playful gestures, even her tears—are executed with precision, care and one-pointed focus.

I remember an interesting story that illustrates this truth. In 2003, a director named Jan Kounen came to the āśram in order to make a documentary about Amma. This was the year of Amma's 50th birthday, and he wanted to film the massive darśan sessions that took place during the days surrounding the holiday. Now, on such occasions, Amma can give darśan to as many as 2,000 people per hour. To witness such a thing is really something. Two lines of people—one coming from Amma's right and one coming from her left. A dual conveyor belt of love. Reflecting on filming this, Kounen said, "She was going so fast! At first the eye doesn't catch it. It just looks disorganized, like a blur. It was too fast. So I decided to shoot her in slow-motion. Only then did I really start to see: 'No, it's not like that. There is such grace and beauty there. Everything is so deliberate. It is like a ballet.'" As if to prove the amount of awareness with which Amma is functioning during such sessions, Amma will suddenly stop and, grabbing a person coming for darśan, will playfully scold, "Hey, you naughty fellow! You came twice!" God only knows how, but Amma remembers each and every face, even in the midst of massive crowds.

That said, we should remember that Amma's mind is already purer than pure. She need not refine it. She has already attained the ultimate. The meditative-ness of her actions is her natural state of being and serves only as an example to inspire the world to follow in her footsteps for its own upliftment.

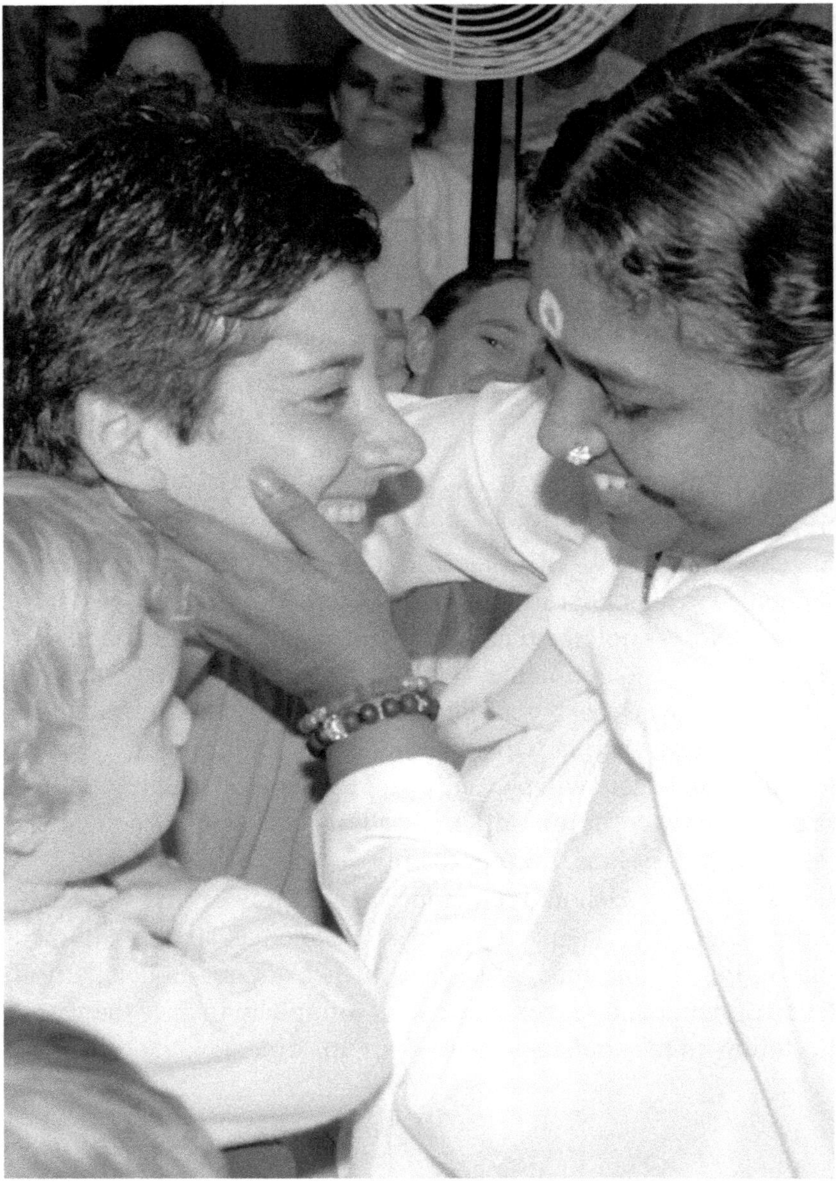

Chapter Nine:

Removing the Root of Sorrow

"Darkness is not something that can be physically removed. But when we let in light, darkness automatically ceases to exist. In the same way, when true knowledge awakens, the darkness of ignorance disappears. Then we awaken to eternal light."

—Amma

THE FINAL STEP in the path to liberation is that of *jñāna yoga*—knowledge. All the other practices enumerated so far—*karma yoga*, *saguṇa* meditation, cultivating divine qualities, etc.—are in fact preparatory for jñāna yoga alone. As discussed in previous chapters, the aim of karma yoga is to help us reduce our likes and dislikes, thoughts which distract our mind by pulling it in various directions. Saguṇa meditation is aimed at increasing the mind's power of concentration. To summarize, if we think of the spiritual journey as taking place on a rocket, meditation increases the power of the rocket's engine and karma yoga makes the ship more aerodynamic. There is only one thing missing in this metaphor: the destination. *Ātma jñāna*—Self-knowledge—is the destination. In order to reach this destination we have to undergo a very strange journey. It's strange because we only reach the destination when we've come to understand that we were already there to begin with! From this statement alone we can see just how subtle a knowledge ātma jñāna is, and therefore just how important are the two-fold mental refinements born out of karma yoga and meditation.

There is only one reason people take to spirituality, and that is because they are not as happy as they would like to be. In fact, as previously discussed, it is the desire for happiness, or more happiness, or the fear of losing whatever happiness we currently have that drives our entire lives. We get jobs because we know we need money to fulfill at least our basic survival needs such as food, clothing and shelter. We go to the movies and listen to music and seek out relationships because we believe they will enrich us. Even our adherence to morality, social codes and selfless actions are aimed at establishing and maintaining a sense of inner peace and fulfillment. These things bring us various degrees of temporary happiness, but it is always mixed with sorrow. Most people in the world continue living in this fashion, hoping that one day they will somehow find the perfect arrangement wherein they live happily ever after—the pot of gold at the end of the rainbow. Or they simply become 'content being discontent.' They come to understand that life will always be a mix of ups and downs and decide to suffer the downs for the joy of the intermittent ups.

Most people are willing to accept 90 percent sorrow for just 10 percent happiness. The strange thing is that they would never accept such inefficiency with regards to anything else in life. Can you imagine keeping a car that started only once every 10 days? The crux of the problem is that they really see no other choice available to them.

Spiritual masters like Amma are here to let us know that there is another choice: Self knowledge—realizing one's true nature. They tell us that only through knowing who we truly are will we gain all the happiness we are longing for in life. This is because the temporary happiness, bliss and joy we experience through fulfilling our desires is in fact welling up from within alone. If we come to identify with that source, we will never again know even a raindrop of sorrow.

Right now I can confidently guess one of the happiest moments in your life. Imagine it's 10:00 p.m. and you retire for the night.

You have to wake up at 5:00 a.m. to get to work on time, so you set your alarm. Soon you are deep asleep. The next thing you know, for some reason, you're awake. The room is pitch black. You cannot see anything, and you are not sure what time it is. It could be that you've only been sleeping an hour or so. Or it could be 4:59 a.m.! Saying a quick prayer, you reach to the nightstand beside your bed and feel around for the alarm clock. You find it, take it in your hand and bring it before your eyes. You say one more quick prayer and then hit the clock's light button. What do you see? 11:30 p.m.! Yes! Five and a half more hours of sleep! That is perhaps the happiest moment of our lives.

What is this all about? There is no delicious food in deep sleep. There are no beach-side resorts, no supermodels, no money, no name or fame. There aren't even dreams. Just nothingness. Yet, somehow, upon waking, we know that there is nothing more blissful. The saints and sages say the memory of this deep-sleep experience—of remembering nothing but that we were blissful—is proof that all happiness is coming from within us alone. It is only our desires that obstruct it. I remember someone once asked Amma what being Self-realized was like, and Amma said, "It's like experiencing the bliss of deep sleep, only that you are wide awake."

In Self-realization we come to abide in that bliss eternally, regardless of what happens in the outside world. It is, in Amma's own words, "a feeling of complete fullness, with absolutely nothing else to gain in life—a realization that makes life perfect." This is what we, as spiritual seekers, are after. And it is only through knowledge—true understanding regarding who we are and what we are not—that we will attain it.

KNOWING THE KNOWER

Knowing the ātma happens to be a bit tricky because it is not an object. That is why Self knowledge is considered the most subtle of all branches of knowledge. With anything else we study, the thing we are learning about is an object. For example, in astronomy, 'I,' the subject, study objects of astral bodies. In geology, 'I,' the subject, study rock objects. In chemistry, 'I' study chemicals, etc. But in Self knowledge what is studied is the subject itself. And the subject can never become an object for us to comprehend with our intellect. The observer can never become the observed. Can an eye see itself? Does the tongue taste the tongue? Not possible.

In order to explain this, I have heard the following example: One day there is a power outage. Suddenly finding himself in the dark, a man reaches for his flashlight. He switches it on, and the beam issues forth, illuminating the room. The beam is so strong that the man is really impressed. "Wow! What a strong and powerful beam of light!" he says to himself. "The batteries in this flashlight must be incredible!" Wanting to know the brand of the flashlight's batteries, the man then decides to remove them and shine the flashlight upon them. Of course, as soon as he does so, he realizes his foolishness.

So, nothing we've studied in the past is like this. The ātma is not audible like music, so our ears cannot hear it. It is not something with form or shape, so our eyes are useless to reveal it to us. Similarly it has no smell, taste or feel. It is not an object at all. It is the subject. After all, ātma literally means 'self.'

With all other things we learn about, we can then go out and experience them. That is the typical order. For example, we read a book about Jupiter. The book tells us how to find it with the telescope and then we wait for darkness to fall, go up on our roof, set the telescope in the right position. Then we see it and experience it. Similar is the case with music. Maybe we read about some form of music in the newspaper that we've never heard of before. It somehow interests us, so naturally we then want to experience it. So what do we do? We get on the Internet, purchase some mp3 files, download them and listen. This is the order in objective knowledge: first we learn about it, *then* we experience it.

But Self knowledge, subjective knowledge, is not like that at all. Because, after all, the focus of the knowledge is *you*, your very self. Imagine reading about human beings in the newspaper and then thinking, 'Wow, these humans sound really interesting. I sure would like to meet one!' and then running outside to search for one. It's a ridiculous idea, right? So with Self knowledge we are learning about something that we are already 'experiencing[1],' something you are 'experiencing' right here and now—as you read this sentence. It is you! How can you ever not be 'experiencing' it? So our problem is not one of 'experiencing'; it is a problem of understanding, of recognition—of knowledge.

Let me give you an example. I am sure most of you are familiar with the *Star Wars* movies. They are famous all over the world, including in India. To be honest I myself haven't seen them, but one devotee who is quite an aficionado told me about the following incident. In the second movie, *The Empire Strikes Back*, there is a scene where the main character, Luke Skywalker, is searching for his guru, Yoda. In order to study with him, Luke has traveled to a distant planet. The problem is that Luke has never met Yoda before. He doesn't even know what he looks like. Having landed on the strange planet, he meets this pestering, funny little green creature with big ears. Luke is impatient to track down his guru and become his disciple. But the little green creature keeps pestering him and delaying him and irritating him in general. Finally Luke becomes so frustrated that he starts shouting, throwing things and cursing his fate. It is at this point that the little green creature reveals himself to in fact be the very Yoda for whom Luke is searching. So, Luke didn't lack 'Yoda experience.' What he lacked was 'Yoda knowledge.' It is the same thing with us and the ātma. We are 'experiencing' the ātma right now. We always have been and always will be. We just need someone to introduce

[1] Technically, 'experiencing' is not the right word because 'experiencing' indicates an object being experienced. However Amma and other mahātmas often use the word due to the limitations of language.

us. This is the role of the guru. The guru holds up the mirror of the scriptural teachings so we can see our own face. In this way, he introduces us to our own Self.

The problem is that even though we are currently 'experiencing' the Self, we are also experiencing many other things as well—the inner and outer world. On top of that, we keep confusing the things taking place in the inner world—our emotions, memories, thoughts and ego—with the Self. It is so subtle a distinction that only through the help of the guru and the scriptures dealing with Self knowledge can we hope to separate them. Amma often uses the example of a pile of sugar mixed with sand. She says for a man to separate them by hand would be extremely difficult and time-consuming, next to impossible. However an ant can easily do it. Here, the man represents someone with a dull, unrefined intellect, the ant represents someone who has refined his intellect through spiritual practices and Vedāntic study with the help of a living master. Amma refers to such a mind as *viveka buddhi*—a discriminating intellect.

In order to separate the sugar from the sand, so to speak, the scriptures provide us with many systematic methods. These methods are extremely logical and intellectually satisfying. Some of these include *pañca-kośa viveka*—discriminating between the five layers of the human persona; *śarīra-traya viveka*—discriminating between the three bodies; *avastha-traya viveka*—discriminating between the three mental states; and *dṛg-dṛśya viveka*—discriminating between the perceiver and the perceived. These are all different methods of Self-analysis. We can use a general term to refer to all of these, and that is *ātma-anātma viveka*—discriminating between the ātma and the anātma, discriminating between the True Self and that which is not the True Self.

Through these methods, we come to realize that all the things we thought we were—the body, emotional mind and intellect—in fact, we are not. The essential nature of a thing is its characteristics that never change. For example, scientists define the essential nature of water as H_2O—a molecule that is two atoms hydrogen and one atom oxygen. If you change that formula even a little—H_3O or HO_2, for example—you no longer have water. But must H_2O be a liquid? No, it can be frozen and it is still water. So, too, it can be in vapor form. It can also take any shape—pour it into a round goblet or into a skinny flute or even freeze it into the form of an elephant and put it as a decoration as part of a big brunch buffet. None of these modifications change its essential nature of H_2O. It is still water. Take it to India, to Spain, Japan or England... no problem. Call it *pāni, agua, mizu,* water or even make up your own word for it. As long as it is H_2O, it is the same thing.

If we look at the body, mind and intellect, we see that they are always changing. Our height and weight are ever fluctuating. We may even go to war and come back missing a limb. Our I.Q. changes. So, too, our likes and dislikes. Food we hated as a child, today we relish. We can love someone one moment and hate them the very next. Our intellectual convictions regarding things such as religion, politics, right and wrong—all change. Our jobs change, the places we live change... In today's world even someone's gender can change. This means that the body, emotions and intellect are all superficial aspects of our being. They are not the unchanging essence—the ātma.

Ask someone who he is and he will only give you descriptions regarding his body. He will perhaps say things like: "I am a man," "I am 56 years old," "I am the son of so and so," "I work at such-and-such factory." If we look at all these statements, there is only one thing that does not ever change: the 'I.' The 'I' is constant. And the scriptures tell us if we go deep on this 'I,' we will see that at its heart is our true nature. As Amma says, "That nameless, formless, all-pervasive principle common in all as the 'I' is the ātma, Brahman or God."

THE NATURE OF CONSCIOUSNESS

The ātma is referred to by many names—*brahman, puruṣa, paramātma, prajña, caitanyam, nirguṇa īśvara*—but as the Vedas themselves say, *ekaṁ sat viprāḥ bahudhā vadanti*—'Truth is one, sages call it variously.'[2] And all these words we've listed in essence mean 'pure consciousness.' Consciousness is our true nature. We learn through the scriptures that consciousness is not something related to the body or mind or produced by the body or mind, yet it pervades them, illumines them and gives them life. Its nature in the body is that of the witness, witnessing all our thoughts, feelings, emotions, as well as their absence. Therefore the scriptures say:

> yanmanasā na manute yenāhurmano matam |
> tadeva brahma tvaṁ vidhi nedaṁ yadidam-upāsate ||

> *"That which cannot be apprehended by the mind, but by which, they say, the mind is apprehended—That alone know as Brahman and not that which people here worship."* [Kena Upaniṣad, 1.6]

In fact, consciousness is not limited by the boundaries of the body. It only seems to be because consciousness, being so subtle, is only perceivable when it has a reflecting medium, such as the body or mind. To explain this phenomenon, the example of light is often used.[3] We can only 'see' light when it bounces off something—a wall, a face, a hand, etc. This is why outer space—where there are no objects for light to reflect against—appears black, i.e. devoid of light. Yet light certainly is there. The sun's rays that illumine life on earth must pass through outer space in order to reach here. But as there is no reflecting medium, we cannot see them. It is the

[2] Ṛg Veda, 1.164.46

[3] Throughout India, light is used to symbolize consciousness because both illumine what is otherwise hidden.

same with consciousness. As stated earlier, consciousness itself can never be an object for our perception. We only can perceive it when it reflects off some medium—like the body and mind.

Consciousness is also said to be eternal—with no beginning and no end. In fact it is the only eternal thing. And as it is not inherently related to the body, it of course continues to exist after the body dies. Why then do bodies seem to become devoid of consciousness upon one's demise? Again, it is because there is no longer a proper medium to reflect consciousness.

This does not mean consciousness is no longer there. To explain this, Amma often gives the example of a ceiling fan. She says, "When a light bulb burns out or a fan stops turning, it doesn't mean there is no electricity. When we stop fanning ourselves with a hand-held fan, the flow of air stops, but this doesn't mean that there's no air. Or when a balloon bursts, it doesn't mean that the air that was in the balloon ceases to exist. It is still there. In the same way, consciousness is everywhere. God is everywhere. Death occurs, not because of the absence of the Self, but because of the destruction of the instrument known as the body. At the time of death, the body ceases to manifest the consciousness of the Self. So death marks the breakdown of the instrument, and not any imperfection in the Self."

Consciousness must continue to pervade the body after it dies because the scriptures say it is all-pervasive. The truth is that we are not a human body endowed with consciousness, but rather consciousness endowed with a human body.

To explain this, the scriptures often use the example of total space versus the 'space within a pot.' Space pervades the entire cosmos. Yet if we take a clay pot, we suddenly start referring to the space inside the pot as something separate—'pot space.' In reality, the term has no meaning. It is the pot that is in space, not the space that is in the pot. To prove this, just smash the pot against the ground. Then where is the 'pot space'? Can you even really say it 'merged' with the total space? No, there was always only one space to begin with. So too it is with consciousness. It is all-pervasive. Currently we experience it as being associated with our small bodies, but this is not the ultimate reality.

Science has traditionally considered consciousness to be a product of matter. It believes that when oxygen flows through the blood and revs up the complex and mysterious system referred to as the brain, a conscious being emerges. Along with this comes the fear that when the oxygen stops flowing through the blood, and the brain sputters to a stop, out go the lights and the conscious being disappears for good. But the saints and sages have always said the exact opposite: it is not that consciousness is a product of matter, but that matter is a product of consciousness. To put it another way: matter is not the substratum of consciousness, *consciousness is the substratum of matter.* And with the advent of quantum physics, some scientists are beginning to investigate this assertion. One such scientist, a theoretical nuclear physicist named Dr. Amit Goswami, working at the University of Oregon in the United States, has published studies wherein he states, "All the paradoxes of quantum physics can be solved if we accept consciousness as the ground of being."

This takes us to our next point. If consciousness is all-pervasive like space, then isn't the consciousness behind my thoughts and feelings the one and the same consciousness behind the thoughts and feelings of all the other beings in the universe? And if there is such a thing as God—the creator, sustainer and destroyer of the universe—wouldn't my consciousness and his consciousness be the same? And, finally, the ultimate: in reality consciousness does not only pervade the universe, it verily is the universe. That is, that consciousness itself is the ultimate building block, as it were, of the cosmos. These are some of the main principles of Vedānta, which, just like any other principles, require time, effort and prolonged study to properly learn and assimilate.

THREE PHASES OF VEDĀNTIC STUDY

The study of Self knowledge is divided into three steps. These are called *śravaṇa, manana* and *nididhyāsana*—respectively, listening to the teaching, clearing one's doubts regarding the teaching and assimilating the teaching.

ŚRAVAṆA

Śravaṇa literally means 'hearing.' So the first step is hearing the spiritual knowledge. It does not say 'reading.' Why hearing and not reading? Because hearing requires a living guru. And the scriptures themselves say that a living guru is essential for one interested in Self knowledge. Proper study of the scriptures takes place in a systematic fashion, beginning with the definitions of all the various terminologies and ending with the ultimate truth of *jīvātma-paramātma aikyam*—the teaching that the consciousness that is the essence of the individual and the consciousness that is the essence of God (or the universe) are one and the same. Does a student have any scope for success if he begins his study of mathematics in calculus? So, too, it is with Vedānta. We have to begin at the beginning and move forward from there.

Only a living guru is able to assess the level of each student and how well they are understanding each point. He not only interacts with them during his talks but also before and after as well, as the disciples traditionally reside with the guru in his *āśram*. In this manner, he is able to evaluate where their weaknesses and strengths lie and speak to them accordingly.

As said before, Self knowledge is the most subtle of all branches of knowledge. "More subtle than the subtlest," the scriptures say. As such, our study needs to become a regular part of our daily lives. One cannot state an exact period of time for which one needs to study, as there are different levels of students, but very often people study Vedānta with a teacher in some capacity for dozens of years, if not longer. The scriptures and the teachings of our guru have to become the very fabric of our life.

Amma says that śravaṇa is not a casual listening. It is total undivided listening in which one participates with his entire heart, his entire being. It is a listening wherein the disciple's mind becomes completely identified with the mind of the guru. When this happens the thoughts of the guru literally take place in the mind of the disciple as he speaks. Isn't this the essence of communication?

Normally it is said that to be a guru one must first have been a disciple. This is because Self knowledge comes via listening to a living guru. And where did that guru receive his knowledge? From listening to *his* guru. And where did that guru receive his knowledge? From *his* guru. Such guru-disciple lines—or *paramparas*—can be traced back for hundreds, even thousands of years. In fact, it is said that all true paramparas begin with God himself, as in the beginning of each cycle of creation it is God who serves as the first guru, revealing the teachings in the form of the Vedas.

But in Amma, we have an exception. Amma never had a guru. Even so, the fact remains that Amma has all of the qualifications required in order to lead someone to liberation. First of all, Amma is a *brahma niṣṭha*—a person who has fully assimilated and permanently abides in the ultimate reality of themselves and the universe. Secondly, despite never having been educated by a guru, Amma is able to lucidly explain even the subtlest of spiritual truths. Amma has never studied the Bhagavad-Gīta or the upaniṣads, yet she expresses the exact same ideas found in those sacred texts with utmost clarity and insight. So, clearly, Amma is an exception to this rule.

That said, we should not assume that we also will be an exception. Exceptions are very rare. Once when asked about this, Amma said, "A person with an inborn gift for music may be able to sing all the traditional *rāgas* [modal scales] without any special training. But imagine if everyone else started singing rāgas without any training! So, Amma doesn't say that a guru isn't necessary; only that a few rare individuals gifted with an unusual degree of awareness and attentiveness have no need for an external guru."

A plant may miraculously take root upon dry rock, but a farmer would be foolish to intentionally plant seeds there.

MANANA

The next step in attaining true knowledge is manana—clearing our doubts. A living master is the only external support for a seeker at this stage. We cannot put our questions to a book. If you look at the scriptures, you will see that almost all of them come in the form of question-and-answer between a guru and disciple. In manana we make sure that there is not even one tiny aspect of what we have learned during śravaṇa that we don't understand and accept. The purpose of manana is to make our understanding perfect. In fact, the student should constantly be reflecting on what the guru has told him, mulling it over and over in his mind. Does it all make sense? If not, he has to ask the guru to explain it again. Not only are questions encouraged, they are basically essential. In fact, the disciple should constantly be testing in his life the truths stated by the guru, trying to see if there are any holes in them. His life should become like an eternal science experiment, wherein each time he undertakes an action, he watches to see if the principles taught to him hold true. For only when we are fully satisfied that the teachings are sound can we hope to move on to the next stage: nididhyāsana, or assimilation.

That said, the disciple must have *śraddha*—faith and trust in the guru and teachings. Our testing should be born out of the attitude that the teaching has a divine source and therefore is flawless. Our questions are entirely acceptable, but we should understand that they are due to our own misunderstanding, not due to an error in the teaching. Our questions should come out of the desire to learn, to understand more clearly, not to defeat the logic of the guru or the scriptures. The disciple should understand that the guru is infinitely more knowledgeable than he is, and that if there is a confusion, the problem is on his end. Unfortunately, many of us are not like this.

An IT support engineer decided to join the army. On his first weekend he was taken to the rifle range and handed a loaded weapon. He was instructed to fire 10 shots at the target down the range.

After he'd fired several shots, the word came back from the other end of the range that every shot had completely missed the target. The IT support engineer looked at his rifle, then up at the target, looked down at his rifle again then back up at the target. He then stuck his finger in the barrel and squeezed the trigger. Sure enough, his finger was blown clean off. After cursing, he yelled down toward the other end of the range: "Well, it's leaving here just fine, so the problem must be at your end."

Often our logic is flawed like this. We erroneously superimpose our weaknesses, lack of awareness, and misunderstanding on the guru, his teachings and the spiritual practices he has told us to undertake. When this happens, it is only we who suffer.

As mentioned in Chapter Seven, Amma stresses developing the attitude of a beginner. This attitude is very important when it comes to asking the guru questions. We should come to clear our doubts, not with the attitude of a debater, but with the attitude of a child. Only one with such an attitude will be able to hear what the guru is saying and internalize it. The one who comes to debate will not really be listening when the guru speaks. He will be busy formulating his counter-response. The mind can only do one thing at a time. If we are busy calculating our counter-arguments, how can we internalize what is being spoken at that moment?

When properly studying Vedānta, we will first remove the doubts that come to us. But then the guru will often pose questions to us as well, questions we may never have thought of before. For the sake of playing devil's advocate, he may even take up the arguments of other philosophies. This is all to make sure that our understanding regarding the teaching is firm and unshakable. As said before, we only finish with manana when every single doubt and lack of clarity of ours regarding ātma has been eradicated. Only then are we ready for nididhyāsana—assimilation of what we have learned.

NIDIDHYĀSANA

Nididhyāsana is one of the most misunderstood aspects of the spiritual path. Nididhyāsana means fully assimilating what we have learned and living accordingly. Take the example of learning a foreign language—let's say, Malayāḷam. In the class, the teacher says, "Okay, class, the first lesson today is the word '*pustakam*.' Pustakam means 'book.'" Simply listening to the teacher speak this sentence is śravaṇam. Correcting any doubt about how the word is pronounced or used in a sentence would be manana. But nididhyāsanam is establishing this knowledge so firmly in the mind that the second I hear someone say the word 'pustakam,' I immediately think of a book. That too, every time I see a book I immediately think the word 'pustakam.' Also, if someone hands me a book and says '*pazham*' [banana] or hands me a banana and says 'pustakam,' I should immediately know that he has made a mistake. Only when this happens can we say that knowledge has been fully assimilated.

In Self knowledge we are learning about the nature of our own Self, the ātma. As we discussed earlier in the chapter, the scriptures teach us that our true nature is eternal consciousness and that consciousness is the source of all bliss. Furthermore, the consciousness within me is the one and the same consciousness in all beings—from a tiny ant up to God himself. And ultimately that consciousness is in fact the substratum of the entire universe. If we have assimilated this, then when we think of our self, we should not think 'body, mind, intellect,' but consciousness. When we interact with others, we should not think of them as separate but as one with us, knowing that the consciousness in ourselves and the consciousness in them is one. When we look at the world around us, even though we will continue to see trees and rivers and buildings and animals and cars and mountains, etc., we will always remember that they are in essence consciousness alone. This will reflect in our thoughts, words and actions.

Once, a guru and his disciples were travelling by foot. There were about 40 disciples in all, and they all dressed like the guru, wearing white clothes and shawls. The guru's head and face were clean-shaven, and so were those of the disciples. By appearance, there was absolutely no way to tell the master from his students.

A few hours before sunset, the group stopped to relax. Soon, the guru and his 40 disciples were sitting together enjoying a cup of tea. It was at this point that a lone traveler came down the road. When he came to the field where the guru and disciples were camped, he paused for a moment and watched them. Then, suddenly, he walked over to the guru and offered his prostrations before him. As he lay at the guru's feet, the guru leaned down and blessed him with the touch of his hand. The man then stood up, took leave and continued on his journey.

Watching this interaction, one disciple immediately had a doubt. "We are all dressed the same. We all have shaven heads and faces. And when that man approached us, none of us were showing any external sign of reverence for our guru. How was this man able to tell him apart from the rest of us?" With this question in his mind, he put down his glass of tea and hurried after the traveler.

When the young monk caught up with the traveler, he expressed his doubt. The traveler smiled and responded, "When I first saw you, I knew that you were all monks. But, indeed, I could not tell who the guru was. But then I looked at the manner in which all of you were drinking your tea. For 40 of you, there was nothing special about it—just a group of men enjoying a cup of tea. But when my eyes fell upon your guru, it was as if I was watching something completely different. In fact, the way he held his cup reminded me of the way a mother holds her child. It was as if there could be no object dearer to him in the entire universe. It was as if he was not holding an insentient object at all, but God himself embodied in a metal cup. Seeing this, it was infinitely clear to me that he was the master, so I walked directly up to him and offered my prostrations."

The assimilation of Self-knowledge radically transforms us. Because if we see others as one with us, at whom is there to get angry? Of whom is there to be jealous? Of whom is there to be afraid? Whom is there to hate or fear?

As said in the scriptures:

yastu sarvāṇi bhūtānyātmanyevānupaśyati |
sarva-bhūteṣu cātāmānaṁ tato na vijugupsate ||

"He who sees all beings in the Self itself, and the Self in all beings, feels no hatred by virtue of that (realization)."
[Īśā Upaniṣad, 6]

As Śaṅkarācārya comments, "This is only a restatement of a known fact. For this is a matter of experience that all revulsion comes to one who sees something as bad and different from oneself. But for one who sees only the absolutely pure Self as a continuous entity, there is no other object that can be the cause of revulsion. Therefore he does not hate."

Similarly, if we know our nature to be eternal, what scope is there to fear death? Moreover, if we know we are the source of all bliss, why would we ever chase after the various sense pleasures the world has to offer? We will be complete and content as is. We will still take what is needed to sustain the body—food, water, shelter, etc.—but we will not go to the world seeking out any source of pleasure, security, happiness or peace. We will be, as Kṛṣṇa says in the Gīta: *ātmānyevātmanā tuṣṭaḥ*—satisfied in the Self by the Self.[4]

For various reasons many people believe that nididhyāsana is something to be performed locked into 24-hour-a-day meditation, perhaps in some cave in the Himālayas. But this is not the case. While we certainly can perform nididhyāsana in seated meditation with our eyes closed, we can also do it throughout our life—as we perform our work, as we spend time with our family, as we interact with our friends, as we eat, walk and talk. In fact, not only can we do this, but we must do it. This is what is meant when the scriptures tell us to 'meditate constantly.' As mentioned in Chapter Eight, in many ways Amma's recommendation that we try to chant our mantra "with every breath" is preparing the mind for this eventual constant nididhyāsana.

In nididhyāsana, we are dwelling on the teaching, establishing ourselves in it. So, certainly one can close the eyes, enter a meditative frame of mind and assert the spiritual truths and their ramifications. It is not the specific words that are important but the focusing on a certain aspect of the Vedāntic teaching and constantly deepening its furrow in the mind. Ultimately it is the assertion of, and the establishment of ourselves in, that which we truly are—all-pervasive, eternal, blissful consciousness—and the rejecting of that which we are not—the finite, mortal, grief-stricken body and mind. The nididhyāsana process is only complete when a total switch in identification has taken place—one stops considering oneself as a body, mind and intellect endowed with consciousness instead of consciousness that, incidentally, is currently 'endowed with' a body and mind. This understanding has to come to saturate our subconscious mind.

When we are interacting in the world, we can continue this line of thinking. It becomes like the theme music to our life—a song that is always playing in the back of our heads. I remember

[4] Bhagavad-Gīta, 2.55

once many years ago someone asked Amma how it is possible to remember God while performing actions. We were near the backwaters at the time, and Amma pointed to a man in a small country canoe who was leading some ducks down the river. Amma said, "That is such a small boat. Yet, standing in that small boat, the boatman will balance the boat, row with a long oar and lead the ducks through the backwaters all at the same time. Making noise by slapping the oar on the water, he will guide the ducks back on course if they start to stray away. At intervals, he will smoke a cigarette. When necessary, he will use his feet to scoop out any water that gets in the boat. Other times he will talk with the people standing on the bank. Even while doing all these things, his mind will always be on the boat. If his attention wavers even for a moment, he will lose his balance, the boat will capsize and he will fall in the water. Children, we should live in this world like this. Whatever work we are doing, our mind should be centered on God. This is easily possible through practice."

In fact, when we interact in the world, we can actually use the challenges of daily life to spark within us the Vedāntic truths. Remember, if we have fully assimilated the teaching, we will never have a non-Vedāntic response to any situation in life. We need to always act in accordance with the truth the scriptures express regarding our divine nature, the divine nature of other people and the divine nature of the world. Amma often gives the example of someone getting angry with us and perhaps showering us with some abusive words. Instead of reacting and getting angry, the one performing nididhyāsana will think to himself "If the 'I' in me is the same 'I' in him, with whom is there to get angry? Anyway, his words do not affect my true nature as ātma." If we start feeling lonely for some reason, we should think, "If all happiness truly resides within, what scope is there to feel depressed and lonely?"

Whenever we have any negative mental response, we should counter and destroy it through the Vedāntic teachings we have learned. This is performance of nididhyāsanam while living our day-to-day lives. If truly assimilated, even if we are given an unfortunate diagnosis at the doctor's office, we will not become afraid or depressed. Rather we will take strength and courage through the truth that, "This body is nothing more than a piece of clothing. As I have put it on, now the time is coming for it to be removed. I am not the body. I am eternal! I am bliss! I am consciousness!"

In Chapter Five, we discussed several karma-yoga attitudes that can be employed when performing action. One of the attitudes suggested by Amma is that of seeing ourselves as the instrument of action, and not as the performer of the action nor the enjoyer of the action's results. In fact, when one comes to the nididhyāsana stage of spiritual life, this attitude can still be used when engaging in actions. In nididhyāsana, even while performing actions, we are remembering that in fact we are not the body, emotions or intellect, but pure consciousness. Thus, now when we act, we employ the same thinking, with only a slight modification. We see the body and mind as inert instruments interacting with the world as per the flow of the cosmic energy (i.e. "in the hand of the Lord"), but we ourselves are not the body, nor the mind, nor the cosmic energy, but pure consciousness witnessing all these phenomena.

In this way, our entire life becomes like a test. Each time we respond in a manner in harmony with Vedānta, we are passing. Each time we don't, it is a reminder that more assimilation is required. By responding in harmony with Vedānta, we don't just mean at the physical and verbal level. This is important, but most important is the mental level. When someone insults us, we may be able to smile outwardly, but what is the reaction in our mind?

Two years ago, a very senior āśram resident was diagnosed with terminal cancer. He was 79 and had been living in Amṛtapuri since 1987. His diagnosis came as a surprise to everyone. When it came, the prognosis was clear. He had maybe two months left to live. He moved into a room in the small Amṛta Kṛpa Charitable Hospital located in Amṛtapuri for his final months, during which time hundreds of devotees and āśramites paid him short visits in order to say their farewells. What they saw in the hospital room was a shining example of Vedānta—a cheerful, blissful man who said his only wish was to take birth again without delay in order to help Amma and her charitable mission. He was not at all preoccupied with his body or its disease. Instead he would say, "This disease is offering me the perfect chance to practice all of Amma's teachings." And this is how he spent his final months, blissfully greeting one and all, and constantly reflecting on the supreme truth that he was in no way the body.

In this regard, Amma says, life itself often serves as the guru. But while life may naturally test us, Amma herself will also personally throw us some curveballs from time to time, just to see how on point we are! I remember once there was a Westerner whom Amma had given a spiritual name[5]. This person's primary spiritual practice was along the lines we have been discussing. The name Amma had given her was also very Vedāntic—indicating the true nature of the Self. For the sake of this book, let's say the name was 'Sarva-vyāpini,' which means 'All-Pervasive One.' Then one day Amma decided to name another devotee 'Sarva-vyāpini.' When the 'original' Sarva-vyāpini came to know this, she got wild. She came up to Amma full of anger and tears and said, "When Amma gave me that name, it was like she had married me. And in giving it to someone else, it is like she has now called for a divorce!" When Amma heard this, she couldn't help but laugh. She then explained to all the devotees around her how this girl was practicing Self-inquiry, through which we are supposed to understand the nature of the Self is all-pervasive and that this indicates that the 'I' in me is the very same 'I' found in you. Yet, when Amma named someone else 'All-Pervasive,' she

[5] Upon request, Amma often gives Westerners Sanskrit names of a spiritual nature.

became upset. How can there be two 'all-pervasives'? No way. Some more assimilation was apparently required.

For full assimilation, there should be no gap whatsoever between our knowledge of who we are and our thoughts, words and actions. If we return to the example of learning a foreign language, then we can say that one can only be said to have mastered a language when they can speak fluently with one and all—the words flowing effortlessly off their tongue. In such a person there is no need to stop and flip through the phrase book. There is no mental formulation of the sentence first in their mother tongue and then mental translation of it into the new language before speaking. It is an effortless, continuous flow. This is how it must become with Self knowledge. In fact when one truly masters a language—and it even replaces their mother tongue—they will even dream in that language. Similarly, nididhyāsana is supposed to culminate in an awareness of our true nature that is maintained not only in the waking state but also in the dream state. It should even be there during deep sleep! Amma says that this is her experience—that even when she is sleeping, she simply witnesses her mind sleeping.

HOW TO DETERMINE OUR PROGRESS

Amma says there are only two ways we can determine our spiritual progress: our ability to maintain mental equanimity in challenging situations and the amount of compassion that wells up in our hearts at the sorrows of others. This is because these are the direct results of assimilating the two core Vedāntic teachings—the first being understanding our true nature to be consciousness, the second being understanding that the same consciousness within us is the consciousness in all others.

If I have properly assimilated the first teaching, then no matter what happens in life I won't become stressed. Our bank balance can crash, our loved ones can abandon us, our house can burn down, we can contract a fatal disease, we can lose our job... whatever it may be we will not lose our mental equanimity because we have fully assimilated the teaching that our true nature is not the body or mind but eternal blissful consciousness. What does consciousness care if it has no money? What does consciousness care if the house burns down? What does consciousness care if the body becomes sick and dies? Consciousness is eternal, all-pervasive and ever-blissful. Nothing affects it. And if we have come to be totally identified with consciousness, we will never become upset when adverse circumstances happen in the external world. Our ability to remain calm when all hell is breaking loose directly corresponds to the extent this truth has been assimilated.

And if we have properly assimilated the second teaching—that our consciousness is the same consciousness in others—we will have compassion for other people. To explain this, Amma usually uses the example of cutting one's hand. When we cut our left hand, the right hand immediately comes to its aid—washing the wound, applying medicine and bandaging it. The right hand doesn't ignore the left, thinking, "Oh, that is the *left* hand! What do I care what happens to it?" No, it knows it is inextricably linked to the left hand—that the left hand and the right hand are of one and the same living being and, thus, it responds accordingly. Or if we happen to poke our eye with our finger, we don't chop off the finger. The finger rubs the eye and soothes it. So, once we have assimilated our oneness with all others, it should only naturally follow that we take their sorrows to be our sorrows, that we take their joys to be our joys. The more compassion we feel when we see others suffering, the more we've assimilated this truth.

Kṛṣṇa explains this to Arjuna in the Bhagavad-Gīta when he says:

> ātmaupamyena sarvatra samaṁ paśyati yor'juna |
> sukhaṁ vā yadi vā duḥkhaṁ sa yogī paramo mataḥ ||

"That yogi, O Arjuna, is regarded as the supreme, who judges pleasures or pain everywhere, by the same standard as he applies to himself." [Bhagavad-Gīta, 6.32]

In fact Amma says that as part of our assimilation practice we should at least respond *externally* in a Vedāntic fashion. That means that even if we do not feel compassionate, we should act compassionately. Maybe we don't truly feel the pain of someone who is undergoing suffering, but we should act as if we do—helping them in any and every possible way. Amma says that acting expansively will gradually help make our minds expansive. No doubt this is one of the motivations behind Amma's selfless-service projects. Amma cares about helping the poor, the sick and the suffering, but she also wants to create opportunities for her disciples and devotees to engage in activities that will help transform their minds.

ACTION VS. INACTION

Many people erroneously believe that in jñāna yoga one is supposed to abandon all actions. Even in ancient times, this confusion was there. In the Gīta itself, Śrī Kṛṣṇa clearly says this to Arjuna:

kim karma kim-akarmeti kavayo'pyatra mohitāḥ |

"What is action? What is inaction? As to the answer, even wise men are confused."

[Bhagavad-Gīta, 4.16]

Kṛṣṇa then goes on to explain that what is meant by "giving up actions" is giving up the idea that one is the body-mind complex—not literally attempting to abstain from action. Kṛṣṇa explains this through a verse that sounds a bit like a riddle:

karmaṇya karma yaḥ paśyedakarmaṇi ca karma yaḥ |
sa buddhimān-manuṣyeṣu sa yuktaḥ kṛtsna-karma-kṛt ||

"He who sees inaction in action, and action in inaction, he is wise among men, he is a yogi and accomplisher of everything." [Bhagavad-Gīta, 4.18]

The meaning is that one with spiritual understanding knows that, even though the body acts and the mind thinks, consciousness—one's true nature—remains ever actionless. And conversely he understands that even though one may appear actionless—i.e. during sleep, meditation or when otherwise sitting still—as long as he still identifies with his mind and body, he has yet to transcend action.

Then, with regards to the meaning of the type of actionlessness sought in spiritual life, Kṛṣṇa concludes:

karmaṇyabhipravṛttopi naiva kiṁcit-karoti saḥ ||

"Though engaged in karma, verily [the sage] does not do anything." [Bhagavad-Gīta, 4.20]

The misconception that the culmination of spiritual life is sitting around in some catatonic-like state or generally being a good-for-nothing is something that Amma has been vehemently trying to eradicate throughout her life. She does this through her talks, where she regularly mocks so-called Vedāntins who proclaim *aham brahmāsmi*—'I am Brahman'—yet complain if they don't get their meals and tea on time. She refers to such Vedāntins as 'bookworm Vedāntins.' Not only is their knowledge limited to books, but they also destroy the spirit of those very books via their hypocrisy. A true Vedāntin, as the saying goes, should 'not only talk the talk, but walk the walk.'

Without the guidance of a proper guru, we can easily fall victim to our clever ego and begin manipulating scriptures to suit our likes and dislikes. Once a priest was caught speeding. When the cop walked up to his window, he quoted, "Blessed are the merciful, for they shall obtain mercy."

Handing him the ticket, the cop quoted back, "Go thou and sin no more."

Amma says that a true knower of the ātma will be humbler than the humblest, as he sees inherent divinity in everything. Isn't this what we see in Amma? During Devi Bhāva, she showers everyone with flower petals. Why? We take it as a form of blessing, but in Amma's eyes she is simply worshipping God—offering flowers to thousands of manifestations of the divine. As Amma once said when a reporter asked her if she is being worshipped by her devotees, "No, no, it is the other way around. I worship them." The understanding that 'Not only am I Brahman, but so too is everyone else' is the ultimate source of Amma's humility. This is why we see Amma constantly offering her prostrations—to things offered to her, to her devotees and visitors, to cups of water handed to her, to everything. Unfortunately, we see a lot of deluded seekers becoming more and more arrogant with every upaniṣad they study. This is not the fault of the scriptures but of the seekers. Amma sometimes jokes that to call a Vedāntin who cannot 'walk the walk' a 'Vedāntin' is like naming a cripple 'Nātarāja' or a cross-eyed woman 'Ambujākṣi'[6].

I remember, once a new brahmacāri asked Amma if there comes a point where one just has to make the resolve to stop performing actions or if action would drop naturally on its own accord. As part of completely destroying the young man's misconception, I remember Amma saying, "Śrī Kṛṣṇa never stopped performing actions and neither has Amma. It is not the action that is given up. It is the idea that one is the body performing the actions."

---

[6] Common Indian names. Nātarāja, a name for Lord Śiva, means 'Lord of Dance'; Ambujākṣi, a name for Devi, means 'She With Lotus-like Eyes.'

But more than combating this misconception through words, Amma combats it through her life. In Amma we see one who verily radiates supreme knowledge with her every word, look and gesture. Her knowledge is flawless. For Amma, there is nothing but divine bliss. The mountains, sky, sun, moon, stars, people, animals and insects—for Amma, all are but different rays of light reflecting off the infinite facets of the diamond of consciousness that she knows to be her Self. In truth, if Amma wanted, she could easily close her eyes and ignore the trifles we know as name and form, seeing them to be of no more importance than the shifting forms of clouds upon the infinite sky. Yet she never has, and she never will. Instead she comes down to the level of those who've yet to attain her understanding. She holds us, dries our tears, listens to our problems and, slowly but surely, raises us up. For Amma, such actions are, in fact, not actions at all. Despite dedicating every moment of her life to helping humankind, Amma knows in her heart that she is, ever was and always will be actionless. To Amma, this is Vedānta.

Chapter Ten:

Liberation While Alive & After

"Jīvanmukti is not something to be attained after death, nor is it to be experienced or bestowed upon you in another world. It is a state of perfect awareness and equanimity, which can be experienced here and now in this world, while living in the body. Having come to experience the highest truth of oneness with the Self, such blessed souls do not have to be born again. They merge with the infinite consciousness."

—Amma

ONCE WE HAVE fully assimilated *ātma jñāna* [Self-knowledge], we have reached the culmination of spiritual life—total transcendence of all sorrow. Understanding ourselves to be not the body, mind or intellect but all-pervading, eternal, blissful consciousness, there is no longer any scope for us to suffer from the sundry mental afflictions that are the curse of mankind. Understanding our Self to be the source of all bliss, what is there to want? Seeing all as extensions of our own Self, with whom is there to get angry? Of whom to become jealous? There is no more delusion regarding the world whatsoever. We become ever-free and blissful. This shift in identification should become permanent. Thereafter we can never see ourselves or the world as we did before. Our 'eye of wisdom' has been opened and can never be closed again.

It is almost like those trick pictures—the ones with a picture hidden within a picture. At first, all we can see is the obvious image—say, a forest. Look as hard as we might, we cannot see the man's face amidst the trees. Other people will be standing behind us saying, "What do you *mean* you can't see it? It's right *there*!" But, still, all we see is a forest. We try and try and try, but still we can see only trees. And then, suddenly, we see it—a man's face. From then on, every time we look at the picture, we see the man's face amidst the trees. Then a new person comes and tries to see it but cannot, and now we are one of the group standing behind him saying, "Come *on*! It's so obvious! It's right *there*. Don't you see it?" This is how it is with Self-realization. Once the knowledge is fully assimilated, there is no returning. We are eternally free and peaceful. This state is referred to as *jīvanmukti*—liberation while still alive.

Jīvanmukti is a change of understanding, not of physical vision. One still sees the dualistic world—the mountains, rivers, trees, old people, young people, men, women, etc.—yet the understanding that such entities are but permutating names and forms atop the eternal substratum of pure consciousness is ever retained. It's just like with the 'picture within the picture.' It's not that once we can see the face, we can no longer see the trees. We still see them alright, but the man's face is always there, staring back at us as well. Amma often compares 'the vision' to how one always remains aware of the fact that all types of gold jewellery are in essence gold alone. We have this understanding, yet we still remember the different function of each piece. The toe-ring goes on the toe, the anklets on the ankles, the necklace on the neck, the bangles on the wrists, the earrings in the ears, the nose-ring in the nose. Furthermore, knowing they are all gold, we consider them all as precious and treat them with utmost care. Isn't this what we see in Amma? She sees all our differences and has different ways of relating to us based on our respective personalities and mental conditions, yet in each of us she always sees the gold. Thus in her eyes, each of us is equally precious. This is the vision with which a jīvanmukta sees the world around him.

It is this vision of a *jīvanmukta* that is presented in the Bhagavad-Gīta verse traditionally chanted prior to eating:

brahmārpaṇaṁ brahma havirbrahmāgnau brahmaṇā hutaṁ |
brahmaiva tena gantavyaṁ brahmakarma samādhinā ||

"The oblation ladle is Brahman, the offering is Brahman, offered by Brahman into the fire of Brahman; into Brahman verily he goes who cognizes Brahman alone in his action." [Bhagavad-Gīta, 4.24]

The beauty of this verse is that, through the imagery of a Vedic ritual, all elements of any action are shown to be in essence consciousness alone—the instrument of action (here, the oblation ladle), the direct object of the action (the oblation itself), the subject of the action (the one offering the oblation), the place of the action (the fire pit, which receives the oblation), as well as the result of the action (the merit gained from offering the oblation). We are intended to extend this vision to all instruments of action, objects of action, subjects of action, places of action and results of action—i.e. every aspect of everything that takes place under the sun. We chant this verse prior to eating as a form of *nididhyāsana* [assimilation]—reminding ourselves that the spoon is Brahman, the food is Brahman, the eater is Brahman, the digestive system is Brahman and the satisfaction experienced upon eating is Brahman as well. Millions of people throughout the world chant this *mantra* every time they sit down for a meal, but how many are actually reflecting upon its meaning? With a little bit of awareness, such mantras become powerful means of remembering the glory of our true nature.

AN EXAMPLE TO INSPIRE

Having a living example of a realized soul in Amma is one of the ways in which we, as Amma's children, are very fortunate. Amma's every word and action can serve to remind us of, and inspire us toward, the ultimate goal of life. If a child is raised in a neighborhood where no one has ever amounted to anything, it is very difficult for him to believe that he can amount to something either. However if someone in that neighborhood somehow breaks free and becomes, say, president of the country, it will become such a source of inspiration to everyone living there. It's almost like when Roger Bannister broke the four-minute mile. Before Bannister, there was a general belief that no man could run a four-minute mile. However after Bannister did so in 1954, soon a number of individuals quickly followed suit. So we should never underestimate the power of living examples.

Therefore, simply *seeing* an enlightened being will transform us. And definitely when we see and observe Amma—the love she radiates, the compassion of her smile, the tenderness of her glance—a change does take place. Because we come face to face with the living proof of our full potential. Until we witness someone like Amma, who can blame us for believing the state of Self-realization to be the stuff of myth?

In Amma, we see someone who lives with the full fruit of ātma jñāna—no anger, no hatred, no jealousy, no selfish desires, just compassion for one and all, and peace and happiness regardless of the external situation. These are all direct results of her crystal-clear understanding regarding what she is and what she is not.

TRUE FREEDOM

These days, many people speak about freedom. No one wants to be told what to do. We want to come and go as we please. We want to decide what kind of clothes we wear, how we cut our hair, what type of friends we have, whom we marry, whom we divorce, etc. In one way, we can call having the liberty to make such choices for ourselves as freedom. But are we really free? If we look carefully, we will see that the individual making all those personal choices is no more than a slave to his likes and dislikes.

If our true nature is beyond the mind, then isn't it a bit odd that we are allowing the mind to run our lives?

Amma points out that while we may be 'free' to act according to our likes and dislikes, we are not free when it comes to the way we react to the fruits of those actions. For example, we may be free to shave our head into a mohawk and dye it purple, but when everyone laughs at us do we still have the freedom to decide how we respond? No, we will feel sad, angry, embarrassed, etc. We lack the freedom to respond to ridicule with joy. So, Amma says, our freedom is, at best, limited. A jīvanmukta, however, is free to decide both how he acts as well as how he responds to the results of his actions.

I remember once Amma told a joke along these lines. After seeing some American devotees come for darśan with their hair in mohawks, she said, "Today old people see the wild haircuts of the young people and laugh. Similarly, the young people see the traditional haircuts of old people—like wearing *śikha* [tuft]—and laugh. However both young and old alike laugh when they see the shaved head of a *sannyāsi*! So in spiritual life we should become like a shaved head—offering our self up for the happiness of others."

Only when we attain jīvanmukti and disidentify with the mind, can we truly be said to be free. In that state, past impressions no longer hold sway over us. It's not that we become like some imbecile unable to remember that fire burns. Rather we are able to come to each experience with a fresh, unprejudiced mindset. And what we see in such individuals is that life no longer becomes aimed at attaining things for themselves, but at attaining things for others—about giving rather than taking. Previously we worked for our own material gains. Now, we blissfully work for others. Previously we adhered to *dharma* as part of our path to liberation. Now we adhere to dharma in order to be a shining example to guide the world—to bring peace and happiness to others. As Kṛṣṇa says:

saktaḥ karmaṇyavidvāṁso yathā kurvanti bhārata |
kuryādvidvāṁstathāsaktaḥ cikīrṣurloka-saṁgraham ||

"As the unenlightened act from attachment to action, O Arjuna, so should the enlightened act without attachment, desirous of the welfare of the world."

[Bhagavad-Gīta, 3.25]

In fact, Amma says that she has been fully aware of her divine nature since birth itself, and we see this reflected in the actions of her life. Never has one seen a more dharmic individual. Even as a little girl she was serving the sick and poor, taking as little as possible from the world and giving the maximum. And now today her entire life is dedicated to, not only personally blessing people through her darśan, but also running a multi-national volunteer organization. She is in charge of charitable hospitals, hospices, orphanages, old-age homes, educational institutions, homes-for-the-homeless programs, welfare plans, medical camps, disaster relief... the list is endless. None of this is born out of some vacuous space within Amma that she is trying to fill through performing good deeds, but rather the selfless desire to inspire the world through her example. This is how the jīvanmukta spends the remainder of his life—blissfully striving to serve and uplift his fellow man. When one fully understands that all the bliss he's sought through the outside world in fact comes from within, it does not mean he will stop performing actions. It only means one will stop performing actions in order to gain happiness. Once one understands one's pen is not a mere quill but a fountain pen with its own reservoir of ink, will he continue to dip it in the ink well? Of course not. Yet he will still continue to write. So is the case with the jīvanmukta.

VIDEHA-MUKTI

The scriptures tell us that when a jīvanmukta comes to the end of his life he attains *videha-mukti.* Videhamukti means 'freedom from the body.' To understand this properly, we first need to look at what happens upon death to one who has *not* attained Self-realization.

The saints and sages tell us that the course of a human being's life, and future lives, is guided by the fruits of his actions. Amma says that whenever we perform an action, there are two results—a visible result and an invisible result. The visible result comes according to the laws of society, nature and physics, etc. The invisible result manifests due to subtler laws and is based upon the motivation behind our action. If the motivation was noble, unselfish, then the corresponding invisible fruit will be *puṇya*—a positive result. If the motivation was ignoble, selfish and damaging to others, then it will be *pāpa*—negative. The visible results come, more or less, right away. The onset of the invisible results cannot be calculated. They come in their own good time—perhaps in this life, perhaps in the next—appearing as favorable or unfavorable conditions and circumstances accordingly.

Let me give you an example. If I push a man, the visible result is that he moves in the direction I applied the force. Now, let's say I pushed that man off a train because I wanted to hurt him. In this case, the motive was ignoble, and in due time it will surely manifest a negative result. Perhaps in a future life, someone will push me off a speeding train. On the other hand, if I had pushed the man off the train because the train was about to explode and I wanted to save his life, then we have a noble action, and this will produce a positive result in time. Maybe someone will save me from danger one day as well.

Throughout our lives all these actions are recorded. As Amma says, "During our lifetime, all our thoughts and actions will be recorded by a subtle sheath, which functions like a recorder.

According to the impressions gathered during one's lifetime, the *jīva* [individual] will take another body during which the implications of recorded impressions will be replayed."

These recorded karmas are divided into three categories: *prārabdha karma, sañcita karma* and *āgāmi karma*. Sañcita karma is our entire karma stockpile—good and bad. It includes the impressions of actions we've performed during countless lives. Prārabdha karma is the chunk of karma that is selected from the sañcita-karma stockpile to ripen in this lifetime. It is our prārabdha karma that determines where we are born, to which set of parents, our brothers and sisters, our physical appearance, etc. It also determines when and how we will die. Finally, āgāmi karma is the results of actions we perform in this lifetime. Some of these may bear fruit in this life itself; the balance will merge into the sañcita-karma stockpile upon our death.

If we examine this cycle, we can easily see that there can be no end to it. There can be no talk of exhausting all of one's karmas because one is continually creating new karma every day. So to speak of 'burning all one's karma' in this regard is incorrect. It can never happen. The path of the unenlightened soul is an eternal cycle of birth and death, which is called the cycle of *samsāra*.

The jīvanmukta however is able to transcend karma. The cycle may still continue, but he jumps off it, as it were. This is because he has switched his identification from the body, mind and intellect to consciousness. In consciousness, there is no ego—no sense of being a separate personality who is doing this and enjoying that. Puṇya and pāpa—merit and sin—are only created when one is functioning from the standpoint of ego. So immediately upon Self-realization, one stops accruing new karma.

Unlike the rest of us, upon his death the jīvanmukta does not take another birth. Already identifying with the all-pervasive consciousness while in the body, there is nowhere for the jīvanmukta to go upon death. He simply merges into the supreme reality—with which he was already identified. Even though he may have eons worth of karma left over in his sañcita stockpile, the sañcita no longer has any target to strike. The target itself has disappeared. Upon waking does one have to pay back loans taken in a dream? Of course not. It is similar with sañcita karma upon the death of the body of the jīvanmukta.

This only leaves prārabdha karma. According to the scriptures the jīvanmukta will continue to experience prārabdha karma until his death. To explain this concept, Amma often uses the example of how, even after we switch off the power, the ceiling fan continues to spin for some time. In fact it is only due to prārabdha karma that one continues to live at all. It is our prārabdha that determines, more or less, our time and cause of death. Our final breath comes when it is exhausted. But due to his identification with consciousness and not the body, the jīvanmukta is not much affected by any prārabdha. Physical pain will have to be endured. But knowing that he is not the body, that pain is mitigated to a great extent. Furthermore, Amma says, he has the power to withdraw his mind from the senses at will.

If we look at our own lives, we can see that physical pain is not the largest cause of our suffering. Mostly it is the emotional pain that comes as physical pain's partner—the fear, the tension and worry. For example, let's say that one day while walking home from work we are attacked. The assailant strikes us on our head and steals our wallet. The physical pain is not so horrible. Within a few days we will be better. But the fear can live on in us for years, perhaps our entire life. Or perhaps we become diagnosed with a fatal disease. It may be years before the disease even begins to manifest any serious external symptoms, yet the fear and tension regarding the future can prey upon our every waking hour, destroying our ability to enjoy life. So the jīvanmukta will experience the pain of the moment, but not the anxiety and fear that precede and perpetuate it.

Or if we look from another angle, we can also say that there is no prārabdha for the jīvanmukta. How can we say this? Because the jīvanmukta does not consider himself the body in any way whatsoever. He considers himself to be nothing but eternal, blissful consciousness. There is no prārabdha karma for consciousness—never has been and never will. In fact, to one who has truly come to identify with the ātma, there can be no speaking of 'liberation' nor of 'bondage.' It sounds rather strange, but in ātma jñāna one realizes one was never bound to begin with. Consciousness can never be bound. It was only a mind that was bound, and the jīvanmukta has come to understand that he isn't the mind, nor was he ever. In this regard, the difference between jīvanmukti and videhamukti exists only from the perspective of those who've yet to attain Self-realization. One with ātma jñāna understands himself to be 'free of the body' even when the body is still alive. To him all bodies are the same. He no more identifies with 'his' body than he does with anyone else's. As he sees it, he is not in the body, all bodies are within him. This is what Amma means when she says: "This visible form people call 'Amma' or 'Māta Amṛtānandamayi Devi,' but the indwelling Self has no name or address. It is all-pervading."

This understanding will come to all of us. For this, we have the promise of both the scriptures and Amma. "It is only a question of time," Amma says. "For some this realization has already occurred; for others it will happen any moment; and for others it will happen later. Just because it has not happened yet or may not even happen in this lifetime, don't think that it is never going to happen. Within you, immense knowledge is waiting for your permission to unfold."

There is nothing more precious than the presence and teachings of a living *sadguru* like Amma. In this regard, all of our lives are pervaded with grace. How much we avail ourselves of that grace is up to us. Our 'permission to unfold' is our sincerity—our efforts to tune our minds with Amma's, to bind our lives to Amma's, to dissolve our selfishness into her selfless divine will. When we do this, we find Amma is like a catalyst—accelerating our unfoldment, and encouraging us forward along this Timeless Path.

||oṁ lokāḥ samastāḥ sukhino bhavantu||

"Om. May all the beings in all the worlds be happy."

Pronunciation Guide

"God understands our heart. The father knows that the baby is calling him and feels love for it whether it says 'Father' or 'Dada.' In the same way, devotion and concentration are the most important element."

—Amma

The letters with dots under them (*ṭ, ṭh, ḍ, ḍh, ṇ, ḷ*) are palatal consonants; they are pronounced with the tip of the tongue against the hard palate. Letters without such dots are dental consonants and are pronounced with the tongue against the base of the teeth. In general consonants are pronounced with very little aspiration unless immediately followed by an h (*kh, gh, th, dh, ph, bh*, etc.), in which case aspiration is strong.

a	like the *a* in *A*merica
ā	like the *a* in f*a*ther (vowel is extended)
i	like the *ea* in h*ea*t
ī	like the *ee* in b*ee*t (long vowel)
u	like the *ui* in s*ui*t
ū	like the *oo* in p*oo*l (long vowel)
e	like the *a* in g*a*te (always long in Sanskrit)
o	like the *o* in *o*pinion (always long in Sanskrit)
ai	like the *ai* in *ai*sle
au	like the *ow* in h*ow*
ṛ	like the *ri* in *ri*ver (usually not rolled)
kh	like the *kh* in bun*kh*ouse (hard aspiration)
gh	like the *gh* in lo*gh*ouse (hard aspiration)
ṅ	like the *n* in si*n*g (ṅgṅg is doubling of this sound)
c	like the *c* in *c*ello
ch	like the *ch* in *ch*arm (hard aspiration)
jh	like the *j* in *j*ust (hard aspiration)
ñ	like the *ny* in ca*ny*on
th	like the *t* in *t*able (hard aspiration, tongue at base of teeth)
dh	like the *dh* in re*dh*ead (hard aspiration, tongue at base of teeth)
ph	like the *ph* in she*ph*erd or like the f in fun
bh	like the *bh* in clu*bh*ouse
v	like the *v* in *v*ictory (but closer to a w)
śa	like the *ci* in effi*ci*ent
ṣa	like the *sh* in *sh*ut
ḥ	echoes preceding vowel

Glossary

ahimsa: the practice of non-violence

Amṛta Niketan: an orphanage in Parippaḷḷi, Kollam District, Kerala, run by the Māta Amṛtānandamayi Maṭh

Amṛtapuri: the location of Amma's main āśram, located in Parayakaḍav, Alappāṭ Pañcayat, Kollam District, Kerala

anādi: without beginning

ananta: without end, boundless, infinite

anātma: 'not *ātma*'—that which is other than the Self; that which is subject to change

añjali mudra: a form of reverential greeting, wherein one brings the palms together to symbolize a lotus bud

aparigraha: non-hoarding, refraining from taking what is not essential for one's living. This is the final of the five *yamas* of Patañjali's *aṣṭāṅga-yoga* system

arcana: worship by offering *mantras*. With regards to Amma's *āśram*, the word indicates the chanting of Amma's 108 names and the Lalita Sahasranāma.

Arjuna: one of the principal characters of the Mahābhārata who becomes Kṛṣṇa's disciple and receives the wisdom given in the Bhagavad-Gīta

arthārthi bhakta (arthārthi): one whose devotion is based on prayers for boons

asteya: non-stealing, the third of the five *yamas* of Patañjali's *aṣṭāṅga-yoga* system

aṣṭāṅga yoga: 'the *yoga* of eight limbs,' the name of an eight-step system of yoga enumerated by Sage Patañjali

avastha-traya viveka: mentally discriminating consciousness from the three states of the mind (waking state, dream state and deep-sleep state)

Ādi Śaṅkarācārya: the *mahātma* responsible for consolidating the Advaita Vedānta school of thought. Among his most important contributions are commentaries on 10 upaniṣads, the Bhagavad-Gīta and the Brahma Sūtras.

ādityas: demigods, children of Kaśyapa and Aditi.

āgāmi karma: merit and demerit accumulating by our actions in the current lifetime

ākāśa: the element of space

ārati: a ritual wherein burning camphor is waved before an idol, image or *mahātma*

ārta bhakta (ārta): one whose devotion to God is based on prayers for the removal of afflictions

āsana: seat; a *yogic* stretch or posture

āsuri sampat: demonic qualities

āśram: a Hindu monastery, where a *guru* lives with his disciples; a stage of life

ātma: the Self—the eternal, blissful consciousness that pervades and illumines the mind, body and universe

ātma-anātma viveka: discriminating between that which is the *ātma* (unchanging witness) and that which is not the ātma (all objects that are subject to change)

ātma jñāna: Self-knowledge

ātma samarpaṇam: Self-surrender

ātma pūja: a ritual performed and guided by Amma prior to Devi Bhāva

Bhagavad-Gīta: Literally 'the Song of the Lord.' A text of 700 verses in the form of a discussion between guru Kṛṣṇa and disciple Arjuna. It is considered one of the three core texts of Hinduism.

bhajan: devotional song; worship

bhakti: devotion

bhāva: divine mood

Bhūta Yajña: protecting flora and fauna as a form of worship, one of the pañca mahā-yajñas

Brahma Sūtras: 555 aphorisms written by Veda Vyāsa that contextualize and systematically arrange the teachings of the

Vedas regarding the ultimate truth, one of the three core texts of Hinduism

Brahma Yajña: remembrance of *guru* and Vedas as a form of worship, one of the *pañca mahā-yajñas*

brahmacāri: an unmarried, celibate disciple/student of a guru

brahmacārya: celibacy, the fourth of the five *yamas* of Patañjali's *aṣṭāṅga-yoga* system

brahmacārya āśrama: the first stage in traditional Vedic life, wherein one lives with and is educated by a *guru*

Brahman: the all-pervading, eternal, blissful consciousness that pervades the individual and the universe; the ultimate reality according to Vedānta philosophy.

brāhmin/brāhmaṇa: a member of the priest caste

Bṛhaspati: a demigod who is considered the *guru* of all the demigods

buddhi yoga: 'the *yoga* of the intellect'—a term Kṛṣṇa uses for the attitude of *karma yoga* in the Bhagavad-Gīta

cakra: literally 'wheel'; a plexus of subtle nerves discussed primarily in *yoga*, *kuṇḍalini* and *tantra* systems

dama: sense control

darśan: 'holy vision'—specifically to attain an audience with a God, *guru* or *mahātma*; Amma's embrace

deva: God; demigod

devata: demigods

Deva Yajña: worship of God, specifically in the form of the elements and natural forces; one of the *pañca mahā-yajña*

Devi: the Goddess, the Divine Mother of the Universe, the feminine manifestation of God

Devi Bhāva: a special form of *darśan* wherein Amma assumes the dress and manner of Devi

daityas: demons, children of Ka*śyapa* and Diti.

daivi sampat: divine qualities

dharma: the code of action that takes into account the harmony of the world, society and the individual

dhāraṇa: focusing the mind on one object, the sixth step in Patañjali's *aṣṭāṅga-yoga* system

dhyāna: meditation, the seventh step in Patañjali's *aṣṭāṅga-yoga* system

dṛg-dṛśya viveka: discriminating between the seer (the Self) and the seen (the non-Self)

Gaṇeśa: a form of God depicted with an elephant head, symbolizes either the supreme Godhead or a demigod in charge of removing obstacles

Gauḍapādācārya: the 'grand-guru' of Ādi Śaṅkarācārya. He is the author of a famous commentary on Māṇḍūkya Upaniṣad.

gṛhasta āśrama: householder life—the second stage of traditional Vedic life

guru bhāva: 'the mood of the *guru*'—indicates the role of teacher and disciplinarian

guru seva: performing actions of service as instructed by the *guru* or as an offering to the guru

guru: a spiritual master who teaches disciples

Guruvāyūrappan: a form of Lord Kṛṣṇa installed in a Kerala temple known as Guruvāyūr.

haṭha yoga: physical postures and stretches to prepare the body, energy and mind for meditation

himsa: violence

Hanumān: a divine monkey character in the Rāmāyaṇa epic, who is completely devoted to Lord Rāma; he is worshipped as God by many

īśvara praṇidhānam: surrender to the Lord, the final of the five *niyamas* of Patañjali's *aṣṭāṅga-yoga* system

Integrated Amṛta Meditation Technique®: also known as IAM Technique®, a meditation technique synthesized by Amma and taught throughout the world by the Māta Amṛtānandamayi Maṭh

japa māla: a necklace of prayer beads used for gaining concentration and tallying when chanting mantra

jijñāsu: one endowed with *jijñāsa*—burning for knowledge for the Truth/God

jīvanmukta: one who has attained the state of *jīvanmukti*—liberation from all sorrow while alive

jīvātma-paramātma-aikya jñāna: the knowledge that the consciousness in the individual is the same as the universal consciousness

jñāna: knowledge, especially as related to *ātma*

jñāna yoga: the practice of learning and assimilating the spiritual truths as taught to a disciple by a living master

jñānendriya: (*jñāna* + *indriya*) 'organ of knowledge,' the sense organs (ears, eyes, nose, tongue and skin)

kabaḍi: an Indian sport, wherein two teams occupy opposite halves of a field and take turns sending a 'raider' into the other half. The raider tries to break through and return to his own half, holding his breath during the whole raid.

Kṛṣṇa: an incarnation of God in human form who took birth in Northern India approximately 5,000 years ago

Kṛṣṇa Bhāva: a special form of *darśan* wherein Amma would assume the dress and manner of Śrī Kṛṣṇa

kaṣāya: the inability to attain full absorption in meditation due to desires remaining in the subconscious mind

kottu kallu kaḷi: a children's game similar to Jacks

kārika: commentary in verse

karma: action

karma yoga: an attitude maintained when performing actions and receiving their results through which one transcends likes and dislikes

karma yogi: one engaged in *karma yoga*

karmendriya: (*karma* + *indriya*) organ of action (hands, legs, tongue, organ of reproduction and organ of evacuation)

lakṣya bodha: constant awareness of the goal

Lalita Sahasranāma: a litany of 1,000 names for the Divine Mother describing her virtues and attributes

laya: merging; sleep, an obstacle to meditation

līla: divine play, seeing life as a play and acting it in a detached manner

manana: the second step of *jñāna-yoga*, removing all doubts through reflection and posing questions to the *guru*

mantra: a sacred formula chanted for concentration of mind and as a means of prayer

mantra dīkṣa: initiation into a *mantra*

Manuṣya Yajña: caring for one's fellow human beings as a form of worship, one of the *pañca mahā-yajñas*

Mahābhārata: a massive epic written by Sage Veda Vyāsa, in which the Bhagavad-Gīta is found

mahātma: (*mahā* + *ātma*) great soul, a guru, saint, sage, etc.

mā: a syllable symbolizing divine love, used in Amma's Mā-Om Meditation

Mā-Om Meditation: a meditation technique developed by Amma wherein one synchronizes the incoming and outgoing breath with the syllables *mā* and *om*, respectively

mānasa pūja: performing formal or informal worship mentally

mārga: path

mārmika: a master in the science of vital pressure points

māya: illusion, that which has only temporary existence, that which is changing

mokṣa: liberation

mumukṣutvam: intense desire for liberation

Nārāyaṇa: a name for Lord Viṣṇu

Nātaraja: (*nāta* + *rāja*) 'the king of dance,' a name for Lord Śiva

nididhyāsana: the third and final aspect of *jñāna yoga*, assimilation of what has been learned

niṣiddha karma: actions that are prohibited by scriptures

niṣkāma karma: actions done without selfish desire

nirguṇa meditation: meditation on the *ātma*, the Self, which is without any qualities

niyama: prescribed observance required for a *yogi*—the second step of Patañjali's *aṣṭāṅga-yoga* system

Om: a sacred syllable symbolizing both God with and without form, the essence of Vedas.

padmāsana: (*padma* + *āsana*) 'lotus seat,' a seated posture for meditation wherein each leg rests atop the opposite leg's thigh

pañca mahā-yajñas: the five great forms of worship that according to Veda should be performed by the householder daily until one takes *sannyāsa* or dies

parampara: lineage, especially a successive guru-disciple line

Patañjali: a sage from the first or second century BCE who authored the Yoga Sūtras as well as important texts on Sanskrit grammar and *āyurveda* (traditional Indian medicine)

pāda pūja: ritual worship wherein the feet (symbolizing Self-knowledge) of a *mahātma* are washed with oblations including rosewater, ghee, honey, curd, coconut water and milk

pāpa: the demerit incurred by selfish actions that harm others

pīṭham: the sacred seat upon which the *guru* traditionally sits

Pitṛ Yajña: offering to departed forefathers and taking care of one's elders as a form of worship, one of the *pañca mahā-yajñas*

praṇām: to prostrate as a sign of humility and respect, also showing *añjali mudra* or touching the feet with reverence

prasād: a consecrated offering, any food given by guru

pratyāhāra: withdrawal of the senses from the sense objects, the fifth step in Patañjali's *aṣṭāṅga-yoga* system

prāṇa: the life force, breath

prāṇa vīkṣaṇa: witnessing the breath

prāṇāyāma: (*prāṇa* + *āyāma*) 'lengthening the breath,' indicates methods of breath control used for health improvement and gaining concentration in meditation—the fourth step in Patañjali's *aṣṭānga-yoga* system

prārabdha karma: results of actions performed in the past that have come to bear fruit in the current lifetime

puṇya: merit, the invisible result of actions performed with noble intentions that benefit others

pūja: worship, ritual worship

pūja room: a room set aside for worship and meditation

Raṅganāthan: a form of Lord Viṣṇu installed in a temple in Tiruccirapaḷḷi, Tamil Nādu

Ramaṇa Maharṣi: a *mahātma* who lived in Tamil Nādu from 1879 – 1950

rasāsvada: (*rasa* + *asvada*) 'tasting the bliss,' an obstacle to meditation

rāga: mode-scales in Indian classical music; attachment

ṛṣi: A Self-realized master, often referring to ancient sages who first gave voice to Vedic *mantras* and truths

sadguru: an enlightened spiritual master

saguṇa meditation: meditation on an object with qualities

sahaja samādhi: 'natural *samādhi*,' permanent absorption of the mind in consciousness, based on the knowledge that the essence of everything is consciousness alone

sakāma karmas: actions performed as a means to attaining some material end

samskāra: mental qualities inherent in one at birth from previous lives; Hindu rites of passage

sagarbha prāṇāyāma: synchronizing the breath with the chanting of *mantras*

Sant Jñāneśvar: a 13th century saint from near Pune, who wrote a famous commentary upon the Bhagavad-Gīta

saṅgha: community

saṅkalpa: a powerful resolve; a concept

sakha: friend

samādhāna: one-pointed concentration

samādhi: total effortless absorption in the chosen field of meditation, the final step in Patañjali's *aṣṭāṅga-yoga* system

Sanātana Dharma: a name for Hinduism, meaning 'the Eternal Way of Life,' a life based on *dharma*. Its principles are universal and eternal.

sañcita karma: an individual's total stockpile of yet-to-manifest karma

sandhyā-vandanam: a ritualistic series of prayers and prostrations performed by orthodox Hindus, especially *brāhmaṇas*, at sunset and sunrise

sannyāsa āśrama: the fourth and final stage of traditional Vedic life, wherein one renounces all relations to become a monk

sannyāsi: one who has been initiated into *sannyāsa*, monkhood

santoṣam: contentment, the second of the five *niyamas* of Patañjali's *aṣṭāṅga-yoga* system

satsaṅg: a spiritual talk; spending time in the presence of saints, sages and fellow spiritual seekers

satya: truth, the second of the five *yamas* of Patañjali's *aṣṭāṅga-yoga* system

sādhana: a means to an end, a spiritual practice

sādhana catuṣṭaya sampatti: the four-fold qualifications for Self-knowledge—*viveka*, *vairāgya*, *mumukṣutvam* and *śamādi ṣaḍka-sampatti*

Sādhana Pañcakam: a text of five verses enumerating 40 spiritual instructions written by Ādi Śaṅkarācārya

sākṣi bhāva: functioning in the mood of a witness with regards to both the external world and mental functions

sāri: traditional dress of Indian women

seva: selfless service

sūtra: an aphorism, knowledge encapsulated in short verses

svādhyāya: Self study—i.e. studying scriptures that teach one about the Self, the fourth *niyama* of Patañjali's *aṣṭāṅga-yoga* system

śama: mind control

śamādi ṣatka sampatti: 'the six-fold qualifications beginning with *śama* (mind control)—*śama*, *dama*, *uparama*, *titikṣa*, *śraddha*, *samādhana*

śarīra-traya viveka: discriminating between the *ātma* and the three bodies (gross, subtle and causal)

śaucam: cleanliness, the first of the five *niyamas* of Patañjali's *aṣṭāṅga-yoga* system

śāstra: scripture

śāśvata: eternal, timeless

Śiva: a form of God that symboizes either the cosmic force of dissolution or the supreme Godhead, depending on context; consciousness; auspicousness

śraddha: (Sanskrit) acting out of faith/trust in *guru* and scriptures; (Malayāḷam) alertness with regards to one's actions, words and thoughts

śravaṇa: listening to spiritual teachings, the first of three steps in *jñāna yoga*

Śrīmad Bhāgavatam: the Bhagavata Purāṇa, a text attributed to Veda Vyāsa describing various incarnations of Lord Viṣṇu, including the life of Kṛṣṇa

Śuka Muni: the enlightened son of Veda Vyāsa

tabala: Indian hand drums

tamas: the *guṇa* [quality] of lethargy, ignorance and sloth

tapas: austerity, the third of the five *niyamas* of Patañjali's *aṣṭāṅga-yoga* system

titikṣa: the ability to maintain patience and even-mindedness when undergoing the various experiences of life, such as heat and cold, pleasure and pain, etc.

Upadeśa Sāram: 'The Essence of Wisdom,' a text on spiritual practices and the Self, written by Ramaṇa Maharṣi

upaniṣad: Vedic teaching wherein the nature of the Self is explained; the philosophical portion of the Vedas

uparama: steadfast abidance in one's *dharma*

Varuṇa Deva: the demigod who presides over water, specifically the oceans and rains

vairāgya: dispassion, detachment

vānaprastha āśrama: the third stage of traditional Vedic life wherein one abandons the home in order to live a life of meditation in the forest or in a *guru*'s hermitage

vāsana: mental tendencies, latent or manifest

Veda: The primary texts of Hinduism. There are four in number: Ṛg Veda, Sāma Veda, Atharva Veda and Yajurveda. Each Veda is roughly divided into four sections: the *samhita* section, the *brāhmaṇa* section, the *araṇyaka* section, the *upaniṣad* section. These deal with chanting of *mantras*, rituals, meditation and supreme knowledge, respectively. The Vedas are not written by man, but are said to be revealed by the Lord to sages in the depth of their meditations. Originally Vedas were learned orally. They were only codified and written down 5,000 years ago.

Veda Vyāsa: a very important sage in the history of Hinduism. He is credited with compiling the Vedas and authoring the Brahma Sūtras, the Mahābhārata, the Śrīmad Bhāgavatam and many other important Hindu texts

videha-mukta: one who has attained *videha-mukti*—total freedom from the body and the endless cycle of birth and death

vikṣepa: mental agitation, an obstacle to meditation

Viṣṇu: a form of God, symbolizing either the supreme Godhead or the cosmic force of sustenance, depending on context

viveka: discriminative thinking, specifically the ability to discriminate between the eternal (the Self) and the non-eternal (the not-Self)

viveka buddhi: a purified intellect endowed with the power of discriminative thinking

yajña: a Vedic rite, a form of worship, an attitude behind every action that helps one to attain Self-realization

yama: a prohibited activity, the first step in Patañjali's *aṣṭāṅga-yoga* system

Yoga Sūtras: a collection of 196 aphorisms written by Sage Patañjali, wherein the *aṣṭāṅga-yoga* system is enumerated

yoga: to join, to merge

Yudhiṣṭhira: the eldest of the five Pāṇḍavas, the noble brothers of the Mahābhārata epic

CPSIA information can be obtained
at www.ICGtesting.com
Printed in the USA
LVHW080938200222
711568LV00014B/504

9 781680 370720